What ... others are  World's Greatest Small Group ...

Michael's passion for group life and group leaders is focused, thoughtful, and contagious! Here he invites us to discover the group leadership principles of Jesus...the place every group leader needs to start!

— Bill Donahue,
Professor, Leadership Coach, and Best-Selling Author of *Leading Life-Changing Small Groups* and *The Irresistible Community*

Everyone is looking for shortcuts on how to create a thriving small group ministry. Unfortunately, there are no quick fixes when building authentic Biblical community. There are, however, trusted guides to take us there. Michael Mack is one of the best, and this book is his roadmap!

— Brian Jones,
Senior Pastor, Christ's Church of the Valley, Philadelphia Suburbs; Author of *Second Guessing God*

My reactions to reviewing this book were "Inspiring! Convicting! Energizing!" Its frequent application segments reinforced each of the teaching segments. I sense an anointing was given to Michael to pass on to us through these pages.

— Dr. Ralph W. Neighbour, Jr.,
Founder, TOUCH Outreach Ministries

I've worked on several projects with Michael Mack. Each time it's obvious to me that God has gifted this man with the ability to deepen believers and enlighten skeptics. If you look up the term "small group" in the dictionary, you'll probably find Michael's picture.

— Dave Stone,
Pastor, Southeast Christian Church, Louisville, KY

All leaders are learners! Michael helps you discover, develop and deploy the internal God-given gifts, talents, and abilities that are in YOU to bless your small group. Until you get the vertical connection aligned with God, the horizontal connections in your small group won't make sense. This book will help you and your small group!

- Steve Gladen,
Pastor of Small Groups, Saddleback Church;
Author, *Leading Small Groups with Purpose*;
Founder of Small Group Network (*smallgroupnetwork.com*)

Every year small group pastors ask me, "Rick, what book would be the best book for training my small group leaders?" You're holding it in your hand right now!

- Rick Howerton,
Regional Consultant, South Central Region,
Kentucky Baptist Convention

In World's Greatest Small Group, Michael Mack focuses on some of the most important aspects of small-group leadership: the internal qualities of the leader. While there are tons of important resources to help teach the skills of leading groups, research has shown that the most important determiner of healthy group life is a healthy leader, and Mack's tips help leaders improve in that area. Readers are guided to reflect on their leadership, including their own self-leadership. Looking to Jesus as the ultimate small-group leader, Mack encourages leaders to embrace their important calling.

- Amy Jackson,
Managing Editor of *SmallGroups.com*

For a long time Michael Mack has been a leading voice in small group ministry. Once again he proves why this is the case with World's Greatest Small Group! Practical, simple and Biblical; it's all here.

- Alan Danielson,
Ministry Consultant, Triple Threat Solutions (*3threat.net*)

Michael Mack has for years helped relational group ministry to produce effective leaders and people loving believers. In World's Greatest Small Group he does it again! A great read!

- Jon Weiner,
Community Pastor, Southeast Christian Church

Leading a small group can pull you in multiple directions to the extent that you can start to feel a little lost. In this book, Michael Mack will restore your sanity by showing you how to lead your group with Jesus at the center of it. I highly recommend World's Greatest Small Group to anybody leading a small group or leading leaders of small groups.

– Andrew S. Mason,
Founder of *SmallGroupChurches.com*

Many small group leaders are mistakenly looking for the next great curriculum to transform the spiritual walk of those in their group. But the truth is, curriculum isn't the secret sauce, the leader is. What the church needs today is not better curriculum but better leaders. I am so excited about the release of World's Greatest Small Group. Michael Mack is a practitioner that speaks the language of the everyday small group leader. His content is rich, practical, and will lift the leadership level of every small group leader who gets their hands on this book.

- Mac Lake,
Visionary Architect for The Launch Network,
a church planting network based out of Atlanta, GA.;
(*www.maclakeonline.com*)

What a great resource Michael has given the Church! No matter the size, age, or type of group you lead, Michael skillfully walks you through the highs, lows, ins, and outs of leading a group toward health. Get this book!

- Ben Reed,
Small Groups Pastor, Saddleback Church

As always Mike's Christ-Centered approach to thinking about groups permeates this book. This is a very helpful read about leadership and gives me ideas I am able to implement in my existing system.

- David Flug,
Pastor of Adult Ministries,
Johnson (IA) Evangelical Free Church

Michael Mack is one of the nation's leading small group voices and someone who has greatly impacted me and my small group ministry! Michael's work is always practical, insightful, and thought provoking! The "7 Powerful Traits" that Michael unlocks in this book are exactly what every pastor and small group point person need to truly be a "Life Changing Leader!"

- Derek Olson,
Communications Director at Small Group Network
(*www.SmallGroupNetwork.com*)

I've been watching Michael Mack help small group ministry leaders (and their leaders) for more than thirty years now. What I love about this new book is that it brings together all of the wisdom he's gained with experience. These are not sociological theories about small groups or just the latest fad in groups—these are time-tested ideas that are sound advice for anyone leading a group. I'm planning to purchase a copy for all of my leaders.

- Rick Lowry,
Spiritual Growth Pastor,
1st Church of Christ, Burlington, KY

Practical, readable advice for any current or would-be small group leader. Read this book for yourself. Provide this book for everyone in your church who is or should be leading a small group!

- Mark Taylor,
Publisher, Christian Standard and The Lookout

The influence of a God-centered small group leader cannot be overstated. Even Jesus personally invested in only a handful of men and women. We should do the same. One thing I love about this book—it dives beneath the tactics and digs into the heart of the leader. Michael Mack is a perfect guy to help us explore this territory, since he personifies true servanthood. His passion for small groups comes through powerfully in this practical and relevant book.

- Kent Evans,
Executive Director,
Manhood Journey (*www.manhoodjourney.org*)

Mike is great at making complicated things simple, and this book is the latest example. We're supposed to follow Jesus in everything we do; why wouldn't we look at his group of disciples to see what we should be doing?

- Micah Odor,
Groups Guy, Whitewater Crossing Christian Church,
Cincinnati, OH

Michael Mack knows the ins and outs of groups from every angle. This book is not about the nuts and bolts of small group ministry. It is about the heart of the leader. Skills and strategies can be learned but only God can cultivate a heart. Drawing from Scripture, Michael points the way to draw near to God and become the leader he wants people to be.

-Allen White,
author, *Exponential Groups* (rel. Jan. 2017).
(*www.allenwhite.org*)

Michael Mack is a voice I always turn to when looking for books to help grow my leaders. Few write and understand small group leaders as he does. This book will inspire both new and seasoned group leaders to grow and develop into the leaders God has called them to be. I can't wait for my leaders to dive into this book.

-Nick Lenzi,
Groups Director at Hoboken Grace Community Church,
Hoboken, NJ

WORLD'S

&❤&

GREATEST

SMALL

GROUP

7 Powerful Traits of a Life-Changing Leader

Revised and Expanded Edition
Formerly published as *I'm a Leader ... Now What?*

Michael C. Mack

World's Greatest Small Group
Published by Small Group Leadership, LLC
Pewee Valley, Kentucky, USA

www.smallgroupleadership.com

© 2017 by Michael C. Mack

Parts of this edition were formerly published as *I'm a Leader ... Now What?* by Standard Publishing, 2007. This revised and expanded edition includes the new chapter, "Stand."

ISBN-10: 1539752259
ISBN-13: 9781539752257

Cover and book design by Andrew M. Rector
andy.rector@yahoo.com.

Dedication

This book is dedicated to the World's Greatest Small Group Leader. Many thanks to all the small group leaders and members who have had an impact on my life and this book. Thanks to those whose help made this book possible: Heidi, Andy, Lisa, Larry, Katie, Deidre, Mark, Jennifer, Cheryl, and Susan.

Contents

Foreword

Leading a small group can pull you in multiple directions to the extent that you can start to feel a little lost. You can start out focused until you get busy cleaning the house every week, calling, texting, emailing, looking for the chips and salsa, prepping your study—not to mention actually facilitating your group. Before you know it, you are tired and overwhelmed, trying to figure out why you're going through all of this hassle in the first place.

Remember ... Jesus was AND STILL IS the World's Greatest Small Group Leader. Not only is the process of leading a small group supposed to make you more like him, it's supposed to be all about him. Even when we know that, though, it can still be difficult to maintain that healthy disposition.

In this book, Michael Mack will restore your sanity by showing you how to lead your group with Jesus at the center of it. When your group's hinge point isn't Jesus, you get broken in all the wrong places. When your group is gathered around Jesus, you will be broken in all the right places.

Mike has always been a leader I've looked to as a living epistle. He doesn't just write about group discipleship, he lives it out every day. His insights come from lessons learned in the trenches and time spent before His throne.

Whether you are new to small groups or a veteran, this book will sharpen you in growing disciples from a kingdom perspective. You'll be challenged, recalibrated, and equipped. I think you'll be thankful for it.

Get comfortable. Have a pen and pad ready. Lock in. Enjoy.

-Andrew S. Mason
Founder, SmallGroupChurches.com

Introduction
The World's Greatest Small Group and Its Leader

I came across the "Top Ten Things They Forgot to Mention during Your Small Group Leader Training" on the SmallGroups.com website. One of my favorites on the list was, "Enjoy the journey ... You are now on your own!"

That's probably how some small group hosts, facilitators, and new leaders feel, but I have good news: you're not alone. I've written this book to provide you—whether you are a small group host, facilitator, leader, core team member, Sunday school teacher, small group coach, ministry point leader, or whatever role you currently play—with seven powerful traits that will help you become a life-changing leader. And I have even better news than that: you have the World's Greatest Small Group Leader available to help you lead your group!

I've written this book not because I think I'm the World's Greatest Small Group Leader—I'm not—but to help you learn from and thus become more like the one who is: Jesus. I'll discuss the following seven actions Jesus took as he led his small group for three years, and I'll apply what I've learned to help you lead your small group.

- **Seek** – Jesus' leadership began with his personal relationship with his heavenly Father. So should ours.

- **Surrender** – Jesus yielded his heart and ministry to God. So should we.

- **Shepherd** – Jesus was known as the Good Shepherd, and he is our Chief Shepherd. We, too, are called to shepherd, as his subordinates.

- **Serve** – Jesus came as a servant—to his group and to the world. That's our calling as leaders, as well.

- **Share** – Jesus shared the load and built a team, a team that could continue after he "moved on." What can we learn from him?

- **Steward** – Jesus looked at his ministry as a matter of stewardship. We can learn a lot from his viewpoint of leadership.

- **Stand** – Jesus and other biblical leaders, including Jesus' followers after his ascension, were able to stand against opposition, attacks, trials, and all kinds of tough circumstances. Don't give up when ministry is tough!

This is not a book about the skills needed to facilitate a small group meeting. I won't try to teach you everything you need to know about asking good questions, dealing with challenging people, or starting a small group ministry in your church. My book, *Small Group Leader Toolbox*, available at *www.SmallGroupLeadership.com*, deals with those kinds of issues. This book is concerned more with the internal qualities that make a great leader. My aim is to help you become a leader after God's own heart (1 Samuel 13:14)!

WHAT IS A SMALL GROUP LEADER?

Let's make sure we're on the same page right from the beginning. Throughout this book, I'll continue to define what a small group leader is, but perhaps it will help to start by looking at some potential small group leaders to show what a small group leader is not.

- **Hannah Hostess:** A true small group leader is (or is becoming) more than a host or hostess who opens up his or her home to the group. While this is a very worthy role in the group, the leader has a different assignment.

- **Ferdinand Facilitator:** Hannah and Ferdinand are related. A small group leader is more than just a discussion facilitator. This may be part of the role of a leader, but only a small part.

- NOTE: It's possible you have started as a host or facilitator, and those are great places to begin! Our definition of a true leader moves beyond these initial roles.

- **Billy Bible Scholar:** Billy might be a good small group leader, but his leadership is not based on his superior knowledge of the Bible or ability to quote large portions of Scripture. Remember, "Knowledge puffs up while love builds up" (1 Corinthians 8:1). (This verse provides an indication of at least one attribute you do need as a small group leader!)

- **Lisa Leader:** Believe it or not, leadership may not be the most essential spiritual gift you need as a small group leader. You can use different spiritual gifts to lead a life-changing group, depending on the type, personality, and purpose of your group. God provides each person in the group with spiritual gifts to help the group function. Lisa's job is to facilitate the use of these various gifts.

- **Teasley Teacher:** "Let the message of Christ dwell among you richly as you teach and admonish one another with all wisdom" (Colossians 3:16, emphasis added). In a small group, everyone is involved in teaching one another! As a small group leader, Teasley needs to be more of a shepherd than a teacher. He does not have to be the group's "Bible answer man." Neither do you.

- **Eddie Educated:** While a good education does not preclude Eddie from small group leadership, it also is not a prerequisite. Eddie's heart is much more vital than Eddie's education.

- **Chris "Super-Stud" Christian:** In Jesus' day, the Pharisees were the super studs of the religious world. Jesus' followers, on the other hand, were simple, run-of-the-mill, average Joes. Jesus spent time with some everyday people and made them extraordinary. Chris does not have to be the perfect Christian (whatever that means) to lead well.

Don't forget that Jesus calls unschooled, ordinary men and women to follow him and then turns them into world changers.

WHAT IS A GREAT SMALL GROUP LEADER'S ROLE?

Perhaps the best job description for a small group leader comes straight off the pages of the Bible, from 1 Peter 5:2-4. The writer, the apostle Peter, knew what he was talking about, too. Peter followed the World's Greatest Small Group Leader for several years. Look closely at this passage, and underline the words or phrases that you think describe a small group leader.

> Be shepherds of God's flock that is under your care, watching over them—not because you must, but because you are willing, as God wants you to be; not pursuing dishonest gain, but eager to serve; not lording it over those entrusted to you, but being examples to the flock. And when the Chief Shepherd appears, you will receive the crown of glory that will never fade away (1 Peter 5:2-4).

This passage was written to elders in the first-century church. These church leaders were called to shepherd the churches in a particular city (i.e., the church in Ephesus) or churches that met in specific homes (i.e., the church that meets in her house). This passage also applies to what a small group leader is called to do in today's church.

We'll come back to this passage often throughout this book. It reveals the roles and responsibilities God has given you as a small group leader.

DO YOU HAVE WHAT IT TAKES?

Do you have what it takes to be a small group leader? Depending on your perspective, you can answer this question two different ways:

❑ **NO:** You do not have what it takes ... on your own, under your own power, with your own intellect. That's why it's so vital to remember that Jesus is the real leader of "your" group. "'Not by might nor by power, but by my Spirit,' says the Lord Almighty" (Zechariah 4:6).

❑ **YES:** Don't forget that Jesus calls unschooled, ordinary men and women to follow him and then turns them into world changers. If you follow Christ, the World's Greatest Small Group Leader, he will use you to do extraordinary things. Don't sell yourself short. Say, "I can do everything through Christ, who gives me strength" (Philippians 4:13, New Living Translation).

By God's power, you can do this, but you have to start by first seeking after him. That's the topic of the first chapter.

TALK ABOUT IT

Discuss these questions with your coach, another leader or two, or your core team.

- Who is the greatest small group leader you've ever known?

- What qualities did that person have that made him or her a great leader?

  - ❏ Knowledge   ❏ Love
  - ❏ Facilitating Skills   ❏ Character
  - ❏ Speaking Ability   ❏ Listening Ability

- What did you learn about leadership from that person?

TRAIT #1
Seek

What do you want to be known for? Think about this for a moment before reading on. What do you want people to say about you when you die? What do you want written in your obituary? Jot down some notes here.

I would have responded differently to that question at different stages of my life. As a kid growing up in Cincinnati, Ohio, I wanted to be known as a great athlete, a Hall of Fame baseball player like Johnny Bench or Pete Rose, a great basketball player like the Big O or Dr. J, or a world-class bowler like Earl Anthony or Dick Weber.

My athletic career was not that spectacular. I accumulated lots of trophies, but mostly because I happened to be on some good teams. I did receive three individual awards: one for best defense in basketball—which went to the kid who never scored a basket. In baseball one year, I received the "Most Spirited Player" trophy— which went to the kid who sat on the bench and cheered on the rest of the team.

My favorite award was the Most Improved Player—which went to the kid who didn't stink quite as badly as the year before. The trophy had the initials "MIP" on the plaque. I overheard my mom telling all her friends I received the "Most Important Player" award. At least my mom appreciated my talent!

In college, I would have said I wanted to be well known—period. Didn't matter for what, just popular. I had gotten about as far as I could in most athletics, so just for fun, I tried out for the cheerleading squad at the University of Cincinnati. I figured at the very least I'd get to meet a few pretty girls. On a fluke, I made the squad—three years

In my 20s, I would have said I wanted to be recognized for being successful. I climbed the ladder of success until that ladder—and everything else in my life—fell out from under me.

straight. I was proud to be a "big man on campus" with my cool letter jacket. I was "known."

In my 20s, I would have said I wanted to be recognized for being successful. I climbed the ladder of success until that ladder—and everything else in my life—fell out from under me. That's when I gave my life to Christ, and everything changed. Well, almost everything.

After becoming a Christian in my late-20s, if I were really honest, I might have said I wanted to be well known and successful as a Christian writer, small group "expert," or minister. At times, in my

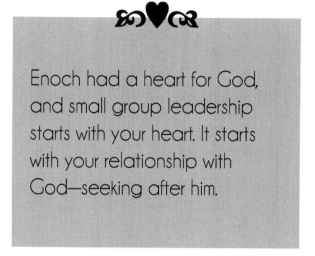

Enoch had a heart for God, and small group leadership starts with your heart. It starts with your relationship with God—seeking after him.

more reflective moments, I might have said I wanted to be considered a good husband, a great dad, and a trusted friend.

Today, I want to be like Enoch.

You don't hear too many people say that, do you? People will say they want to have the faith of Abraham or the power of Moses or the wisdom of Solomon. But Enoch? Who is Enoch?

Enoch was one of only two people who were taken away to heaven without ever dying. The other was Elijah (2 Kings 2:11), who was whisked away to heaven in a whirlwind, accompanied by a chariot and horses of fire. But Enoch just suddenly disappeared. I love what Genesis 5:22-24 says about him: "Enoch lived in close fellowship with God for another 300 years." He enjoyed a close relationship with God throughout his life. "Then suddenly, he disappeared because God took him" (NLT).

No, I don't want to live another 300 years! Neither is it necessary to just disappear without dying, unless it's the rapture, of course. But I do want to live in close fellowship with God throughout what's left of my life, until God takes me when he's ready.

Enoch had a heart for God, and small group leadership starts with your heart. It starts with your relationship with God—seeking after him.

One of the key attributes from 1 Peter 5:2-4 for small group leaders is that you are "examples to the flock." That's why it is so critical that you are, first of all, a man or woman after God's heart. It's why the most important thing you can do as a leader is earnestly seek God every day.

THE INSIDE STUFF OF SMALL GROUP LEADERSHIP

If you were entrusted to recruit a team of small group leaders, what characteristics or attributes would you look for? What would matter most?

- Facilitation skills

- Spiritual gift of leadership

- Previous involvement in a small group

- Bible knowledge

- Daily quiet time

- Relational abilities

- Dynamic personality

- Ability to use a DVD player

- Holiness, piety

- Whoever says yes to joining your team when you ask

How would the World's Greatest Small Group Leader answer that question? I believe he would say something like, "Don't look at the outward appearance; look inside" (ref. 1 Samuel 16:7).

Actually, you don't have to conjecture what Jesus would have looked for in leaders. When he invited some folks to be part of his group, he was calling future leaders. "The plan was that they would be with Jesus, and he would send them out" (Mark 3:14, *The Message*).

The USA Men's Olympic Basketball Team became known as the "Dream Team," as it consisted of some of the best NBA players and a few elite college players. When Jesus selected his team, it was perhaps the most important team ever assembled. Their job: to communicate the most significant message in history to the entire world. It was a

THE WORLD'S GREATEST SMALL GROUP LEADER SAID . . .

"What sorrow awaits you teachers of religious law and you Pharisees. Hypocrites! For you are like whitewashed tombs—beautiful on the outside but filled on the inside with dead people's bones and all sorts of impurity. Outwardly you look like righteous people, but inwardly your hearts are filled with hypocrisy and lawlessness."

—*Matthew 23:27-28 (NLT)*

do-or-die mission. They do it ... or the whole world dies spiritually. But Jesus didn't select a dream team. He called a rag-tag assortment of very average men. And, he said, he would make them into what they needed to become.

If Jesus would have recruited future leaders who looked good by outward appearances, he probably would have picked some of the religious leaders of the day. They were all about outward appearances, which is what frustrated Jesus the most about them. Those leaders had skills and abilities and giftedness. They had more knowledge and holiness and piety than almost everyone around. They were highly disciplined in spiritual practices. But something vital was missing on the inside.

Small group leadership starts with your relationship with God—seeking after him with all your heart, soul, strength, and mind.

GUT-LEVEL LEADERSHIP

The World's Greatest Small Group Leader is a perfect model for us. Jesus' priority was his relationship with his Father. He said and did and

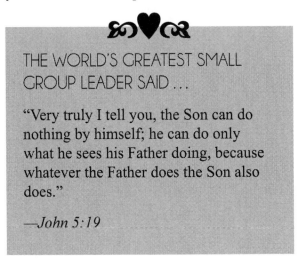

THE WORLD'S GREATEST SMALL GROUP LEADER SAID . . .

"Very truly I tell you, the Son can do nothing by himself; he can do only what he sees his Father doing, because whatever the Father does the Son also does."

—*John 5:19*

taught nothing on his own, but only what his Father gave him. Henri Nouwen once pointed out that Jesus spent about 50 percent of his time in solitude with the Father, about 40 percent building community with the twelve, and about 10 percent "doing ministry."[1] How does that match up with your life?

In *Experiencing God*, authors Henry Blackaby and Claude King also describe Jesus—and godly leaders today—as spending abundant time seeking God. These leaders have discerned the difference between activity *for* God and the activity *of* God. Jesus never ran ahead of God. Instead, before making any decisions or starting any new ministry work, he spent time, maybe days on end, with God, waiting on his Father to show him exactly what to do next.

Pastor and author Joel Comiskey's survey of more than 700 small group leaders in eight countries revealed that the biggest factor in the "success" of small group leaders was not their gender, social status, education, personality type, or skills; it was the leader's devotional life. He found that those who spent 90 minutes or more in devotions (prayer, Bible study, etc.) a day multiplied their groups twice as much as those who spent less than 30 minutes.[2] Comiskey says the correlation is logical. "During quiet times alone with the living God, the [small group] leader hears God's voice and receives His guidance. … Group members respond to a leader who hears from God and knows the way."[3]

Jesus modeled seeking and following God for us. As our Leader and Savior, he is our Good Shepherd who calls us by name and is waiting to lead us (John 10:3-4). Are you quiet and still enough to hear his voice?

Let me encourage you as you read this to get gut-level honest with yourself. Where are you in your relationship with God? Are you …

❑ Walking right behind him; his voice is crystal clear

❑ Meandering along toward the back of the crowd; his voice is like bad cell-phone service—sometimes clear, but with lots of dropped calls

❑ Running this way and that; I hear lots of voices, lots of noise—his voice is indistinguishable

❑ Stuck in a rut; I haven't heard his voice in a while

❑ Other: _____

Before going any further in this book—before considering how you can become a more effective leader—you must get honest with yourself, and with God, on this. Then, there's the next step. You'll need to share this with someone else. Get gut-level honest with another person: someone from your group, a church leader, or a good, trusted friend. I'm asking you to be vulnerable and authentic. Until you get gut-level honest with yourself, God, and at least one other person, you cannot become a more effective leader and guide an effective, growing, GREAT small group!

GO AWAY TO GET INSIDE

How do you get to a place where you can hear God's voice? The only way is to spend time alone with him. I fear small group leaders sometimes miss this vital point. Most leaders are busy people—busy with jobs, families, churches, and small groups. We're all community junkies. We love spending time with other people. But, as pastor and theologian Dietrich Bonhoeffer said, solitude and community go hand in hand for spiritually healthy people and groups.

Jesus modeled this for us, as well. "One of those days Jesus went out to a mountainside to pray, and spent the night praying to God. When morning came, he called his disciples to him and chose twelve of

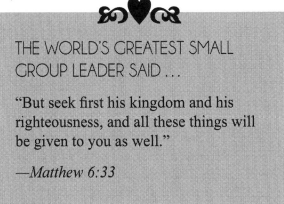

THE WORLD'S GREATEST SMALL
GROUP LEADER SAID . . .

"But seek first his kingdom and his righteousness, and all these things will be given to you as well."

—*Matthew 6:33*

them, whom he also designated apostles" (Luke 6:12-13). Before Jesus did anything else, he spent time alone with the Father. In fact, Luke 5:16 says, "Jesus often withdrew to lonely places and prayed."

Spending time with God is your primary priority as a small group leader. But this will not just happen. You must make it happen! Use the following strategy questions to help you plan your getaway:

GETAWAY PLANNING

- How Often will I get away alone with God? (Weekly, monthly, quarterly, annually?)

- How Long will I spend alone with God?

- When will I get away to be alone with God? (Be specific!)

- Where will I go?

- What provisions do I need to make for getting away? (Asking permission, child care, financial arrangements, place to stay, etc.)

I don't get away for solitude with God often enough, but when I do, I spend a day in the woods, especially a woods with a creek or near a lake. I feel particularly close to God there. I plan on either hiking or taking my mountain bike, but only as a way to get to a solitary place. These times are refreshing to my own soul, they remind me of the calling God has placed on my life, and they revive me for the ministry God has called me to do. More than anything else, during these times, I sense God's presence and power, and I realize that he really is pursuing me and leading me.

On my getaways I take with me only a few essentials:

- my Bible

- a small notepad and pen

- some water and light snacks

I do not take any other books or devices besides my cell phone. I take it only to make emergency calls, but I turn the ringer and vibrator off

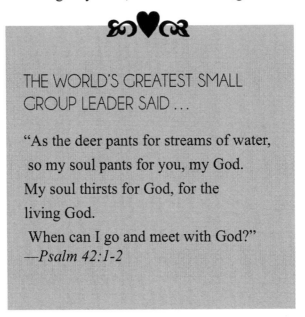

THE WORLD'S GREATEST SMALL GROUP LEADER SAID . . .

"As the deer pants for streams of water,
   so my soul pants for you, my God.
My soul thirsts for God, for the
living God.
   When can I go and meet with God?"
—*Psalm 42:1-2*

and hide it in my backpack so incoming calls don't distract me. I also tell my wife where I'm planning to be and, because I have diabetes, I utilize a tracking devise on my phone—just in case.

Don't miss this! God is either pursuing you, trying to draw you closer to him, or he is leading you, walking in front of you to guide you (John 10:4). When you belong to him, as your Good Shepherd, he does whatever you need at the time.

One of my favorite places is the woods and the creek right behind my backyard. A large boulder that sits in the middle of a stream is mossy and soft and just the right shape for sitting and relaxing. It's an incredibly beautiful spot, where a side stream cascades down a hill.

Lots of flat rocks and little waterfalls create the rhythmic sound of babbling water.

I was sitting there one morning, taking in the vast beauty of God's creation all around me, when I looked down. There, right between my feet, was a little plant growing in the moss. It had tiny white flowers, smaller than the size of the head of a pin, but incredibly beautiful and intricate. I sat there and stared at it for maybe 15 minutes. It was a gift to me from God, a reminder that I needed to look not only at the big picture (something I do a lot), but stop and notice the little things in life, as well.

I had a deadline looming, and I had been working on the project nonstop for weeks. God knew exactly what I needed, and he provided it. He pursued me and drew me closer to him, as I slowed down enough to notice.

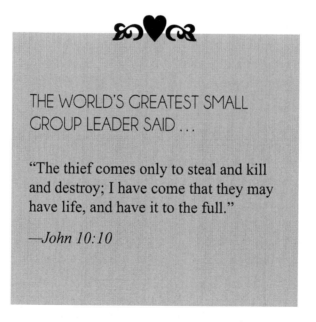

THE WORLD'S GREATEST SMALL GROUP LEADER SAID . . .

"The thief comes only to steal and kill and destroy; I have come that they may have life, and have it to the full."

—*John 10:10*

God desires leaders who seek him earnestly, know his voice, and know his heart—leaders who respond to him and walk in close fellowship with him every day. Leaders like that are ones who are experiencing the abundant life.

LIFE IN ALL ITS FULLNESS

Life to the full, the abundant life, more and better life than you've ever dreamed of, everything you need. These are the ways different Bible versions say the same thing.

You cannot lead a small group to experience the fullness of God's love and grace unless you are experiencing it yourself. In Matthew 11:28-30, Jesus presents three ways to respond to his offer of abundant life:

1. Come to me ... and I will give you rest.

Life to the full comes only through Jesus. Your response to him is to seek God and stay connected to him.

When you come to Jesus, as his first disciples did, you give your life to him, commit to following him, and let him mold you into what he wants you to be. When you come to him, he gives you rest, especially from legalism—following all the rules to be right with God. The abundant life is far more than living a holy and blameless life. The Pharisees worked hard at living like that, but their lives were empty. They were living religious, rule-keeping lives, but not full lives. When your life is empty—when you have not invited Jesus to take up residence in your life—you are in danger of having all kinds of other things—evil things—come in and take up residence. Being religious will not fill you up. It will leave you only empty and vulnerable. Only Jesus has the power to really fill you—to give you life to the full.

2. Take my yoke upon you.

This next step, as you become more mature, is the place of surrender to God. It is not only accepting Jesus as your Savior so you have peace and security about eternal life. This place of surrender is about knowing him as leader of your life and living in surrender to his ways and his will. This is the place of service, using the gifts God has given you to administer his grace in its various forms (1 Peter 4:10). Remember that the "yoke" Jesus gives you always fits perfectly! (I will discuss the subjects of surrender and serving in much more detail in Chapters 2 and 4.)

The abundant life is not the same as the "good life" that so many people run after. It is not necessarily a life free from pain, sadness, difficulties, or the other burdens people face every day. Jesus does not give us these difficult burdens, but he also does not always take away the difficulties and challenges we face in life.

The apostle Paul described how to live life to the full in Philippians 4:11-12, when he talked about learning the secret of being content, regardless of the circumstances. The abundant life is a life of joy—a joy that can be possessed regardless of the circumstances. It is a life of rest from burdens—a rest that only Jesus can give you. It is a life of freedom—freedom from the burdensome, ill-fitting yoke of rule-keeping.

That reminds me of a story I read about a man who was released from jail at 12:01 A.M. At 12:09 A.M. he was spotted climbing over a chain link fence, back onto the jail grounds, and attempting to pass a cigarette to an inmate through a steel grate covering a window. At 12:10 A.M. the man was back in custody, charged with illegal entry into a prison facility and disorderly conduct. True story! Can you identify at all with this stupid criminal? The apostle Paul wrote about all of us:

> Christ has set us free to live a free life. So take your stand! Never again let anyone put a harness of slavery on you. I am emphatic about this. The moment any one of you submits to circumcision or any other rule-keeping system, at that same moment Christ's hard-won gift of freedom is squandered. … I suspect you would never intend this, but this is what happens. When you attempt to live by your own religious plans and projects, you are cut off from Christ, you fall out of grace (Galatians 5:1-4, *The Message*).

What do you allow to take away your freedom? It's probably not circumcision, as it was for Paul's friends. You may not literally be breaking into jail, like our stupid criminal, but all of us, at one time or another, give up the freedom Jesus has given us, choosing to live as a prisoner.

I want to encourage you, leader to leader—don't return to the prison cell of living by a list of do's and don'ts. As a spiritual leader, you are a model of the type of life God wants everyone to live. The Judaizers (those who taught that believers needed to become Jews first by being circumcised in order to become Christians) were spiritual leaders who were not only living as prisoners themselves, they were trying to lead other Christians back into bondage. Be careful, then, not to be like

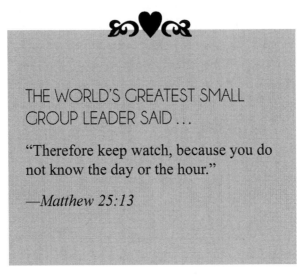

THE WORLD'S GREATEST SMALL GROUP LEADER SAID . . .

"Therefore keep watch, because you do not know the day or the hour."

—*Matthew 25:13*

these "agitators," as Paul called them (Galatians 5:12). Rather, live your life in freedom in Christ!

In Matthew 13, Jesus told his small group a story about a farmer scattering seed on different types of soils. The seed is the Good News of the life Jesus came to give. But many things can keep you from living that life: obstacles, strongholds, worries, busyness, misdirection, and confusion between the "good life" and the abundant life. Jesus gives it freely, but you cannot always receive it. Your heart has to be fertile—ready to receive the good seed God wants to plant there.

Jesus reminds us often in the gospels about the costs involved in coming to him. These involve the possibility of losing your family members, finances, job, position in life, maybe even life itself. How can these "yokes" be easy and not burdensome? Only by putting your total trust in Jesus and learning from him how to live.

3. Learn from me.

Part of the ongoing process of experiencing more of the abundant life is to learn from Jesus how to live. He teaches you by his example, his Holy Spirit, and his Word. As you yield to his will, you learn how to live life his way.

The World's Greatest Small Group Leader lived life to the full himself. So he is a perfect model for us. In John 4:34, Jesus said, "My food is to do the will of him who sent me and to finish his work." Part of living the abundant life is living your life for God, not yourself, doing his will and living according to the purpose he has given you.

In Matthew 24-25, Jesus emphasized and re-emphasized the need to stay alert. The abundant life is lived with a constant focus on Jesus (Colossians 3:2). It's all too easy to shift your attention elsewhere. Jesus is encouraging and warning you to stay focused on him.

When you are seeking him and focused on him, you can live life the way he wants you to live it: abundantly ... actually, superabundantly!

LIVING AN OVERFLOWING LIFE

In John 10:10, the word for *full* or *abundantly* actually means *overfilled* or *superabundantly*. Think of a glass of water filled to the brim. That's what I used to think of when I thought of "life to the full." But it's more than that! It's a life that is overflowing the glass. Your life can't even contain it all! What Jesus pours into your life he intends to overflow into the lives of those all around you—your family, neighbors, co-workers, and yes, your small group. That's why it is critical that you are living the abundant life yourself.

Read Psalm 23, "the shepherd's psalm," with the abundant life in mind. God promises life to the full regardless of the valleys in life. But he promises even more than that. The psalmist says, "My cup overflows" (v. 5).

Of course, Jesus was the perfect example of someone living this superabundant life. He taught his disciples how to live by intentionally letting his life overflow into theirs over time.

For three years, the disciples followed Jesus everywhere. He taught them. Showed them. Modeled it for them. Prayed for them. And as you follow the story through the gospels, you know that these guys just didn't get it most of the time. Oh, there would be a flash of brilliance, a hint of promise, but minutes later they'd look like the "uneducated idiots" that most of the world—except Jesus, it seems—considered them. Dumb fishermen. Scurrilous government workers. Insolent rebels. (In Acts 4:13, the Jewish rulers called Peter and John "unschooled, ordinary men." The word the rulers used for "ordinary" in the original language was *idiotai*. "Unschooled, ordinary men" is just a polite way of saying "uneducated idiots"!

What did Jesus see in these guys that no one else saw? I think he saw potential and promise. He knew that when push came to shove—and it would—that what the Father had poured into Jesus would overflow into the disciples' lives and would eventually begin to flow out of their lives into the lives of others. Jesus staked everything on this.

After three years, they definitely did not look like world changers. But that, of course, is exactly what they became. Somehow, in the midst

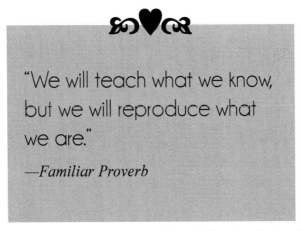

"We will teach what we know, but we will reproduce what we are."

—*Familiar Proverb*

of what seemed like the biggest tragedy of all—the death of their leader—they pulled off what looked like the impossible. The religious leaders, who thought they had gotten rid of the "problem," had a sinking suspicion that it wasn't over. There was something special, something dangerous, about these "uneducated idiots." People were amazed. (See Acts 4:13.)

How did Jesus do it? How were these uneducated idiots transformed? Several key ingredients—prayer, authentic community, and the indwelling of the Holy Spirit, for starters—were involved. And these

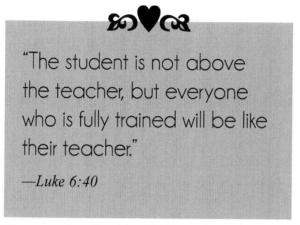

"The student is not above the teacher, but everyone who is fully trained will be like their teacher."

—*Luke 6:40*

are huge, of course. But the thing that people noticed most was that these uneducated idiots had been with Jesus.

The discipline of "remaining" is vital for the disciple's life. Jesus spoke little to his followers about spiritual exercises or spiritual disciplines, even though they were undoubtedly a big part of their religious heritage. Instead, Jesus called them to come and see (John 1:39), come and follow me (Mark 1:16-20), come and be with me (Mark 3:13-14), and remain (abide) in me (John 15:7-8). Jesus did many things in his three-year earthly ministry, but the one constant was his presence with the disciples.

Nothing is more vital to spiritual leadership than being with Jesus—connected to him, remaining in him, abiding in him. Remember that you are not the Vine that supplies all the nutrients for growth and fruitfulness in your group members' lives. You are one of the branches that is dependent on the True Vine, Jesus (John 15:1-17). His life flows into you, naturally overflows into your group members, and then continues to flow from them into their spheres of influence.

When you remain connected to him, you will produce much fruit—abundant fruit, fruit that overflows the containers, fruit that will last. But apart from him, you can do nothing. That's quite a difference!

This overflowing life provides a good definition for a small group leader:

A small group leader is a group member who goes first.

As a good shepherd, you lead your sheep (John 10:3-4). You don't drive them from behind. You lead by modeling the abundant life by ... seeking God

- living in authentic community

- impacting your world

These are the three vital activities that are part of living life abundantly. They are the essential pursuits of every abundant living small group. I will continue to discuss these actions throughout the rest of this book. Your job as the leader is to go first in pursuing each of them, just as Jesus did. Your role is to be an example to the flock under your care (1 Peter 5:2-3).

To live the kind of life I've discussed in this chapter, you must surrender. It is one of the first things you'll need to do every day of your life so you can model it for others. That's the topic of Trait #2.

TALK ABOUT IT

In Ephesians 3:14-21, the apostle Paul prayed for the Ephesian church's spiritual empowerment. Read this passage in your own Bible, and then pray that prayer for each of your group members (starting with yourself).

Pray that Christ will be more and more at home in your own heart, so you are living the superabundant life Jesus came to give—a life that overflows into the lives of your group members. Pray that Jesus will be more at home in the lives of your members, so they also may be filled to the measure of all the fullness of God.

TRAIT #2
Surrender

You are seeking God, striving to live life to the full. The next step in becoming more like the World's Greatest Small Group Leader is not easy, but it is vital. Until you learn to surrender, you cannot realistically live out the rest of the leadership values in this book and become more like Jesus.

The word *surrender*, as it relates to yielding one's will to God, is seldom used in Scripture, yet the idea flows through God's Word from the start. Adam and Eve gave in to sin as they chose their own wills rather than surrendering to God's. Instead, they yielded to Satan's scheme. This pattern has continued to repeat itself through history.

Surrender has been defined as completely giving up one's own will and subjecting one's thoughts, ideas, and deeds to the will and teachings of a divine power or deity.

Some men don't like the word *surrender*. To many guys it means "I lose." But surrender, in the sense that I'm using it here, does not mean capitulation or waving the white flag. It means intentionally sacrificing myself for the good of others. It's *Saving Private Ryan*. It's the firemen at the World Trade Center. It's Jesus at the cross.

SURRENDER YOUR WILL

Living life to the full does not mean getting everything you want. It means knowing and following the will of God. That takes surrender—total abandonment to God, forsaking the security of meeting your own needs by your own means. Surrender demands faith in a God who will never fail you. It is an act of the will.

Jesus provided a perfect example of surrender, first by emptying himself of the privileges, power, and prerogatives of divinity by coming into this world as a human (Philippians 2:7), then by how he lived, and finally by laying down his life for us. Jesus modeled it so we will lay down our lives for one another (1 John 3:16).

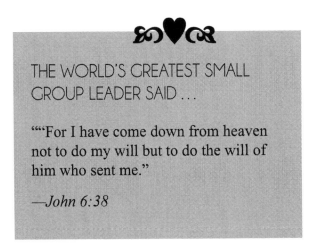

THE WORLD'S GREATEST SMALL GROUP LEADER SAID . . .

""'For I have come down from heaven not to do my will but to do the will of him who sent me."

—*John 6:38*

I love reading through the Gospel of John and seeing Jesus' heart for how he did ministry. Over and over he says, I do nothing on my own. I do only what the Father tells me to do. I say only the words the Father gives me to say. Jesus was voluntarily submissive to his Father and his will. (The authors of *The Ascent of a Leader* point out that *submission* "is a love word, not a control word. Submission means letting someone love you, teach you, or influence you."[4])

At the end of his ministry on Earth, Jesus said he had accomplished everything the Father had given him to do (John 17:4). Up to that point, what had he accomplished? If I had been a reporter for the

Palestine Times, I probably would have labeled Jesus a failure. He was unsuccessful in winning the Jewish leaders and most of the Jewish people over. He didn't cure all the diseases or put an end to any of the regional conflicts. Some expected him to free the Jewish nation from Rome, but he seemed determined not to even try. Even his closest followers still argued over who was greatest, and most of them ran and hid at Jesus' most desperate hour. Yet, Jesus said he had accomplished everything the Father had given him to do.

What you think you should make happen or what others might expect of you may be diametrically opposed to what God has given you to do. What you are called to do is to live a submissive, surrendered life to God, each and every day. As for me, above all else I'd like to be able to say at the end of my life, "Father, I brought you glory here on earth by doing everything you told me to do." That's going to take a change in ownership.

A CHANGE IN OWNERSHIP

In my twenties I worked as a retail store manager. One of my jobs was to go into stores that were losing money and turn them around. The first thing I would do was put two signs in the front window: "Under New Management" and "Now Hiring." I told the existing staff that things were going to change and they would need to work much harder, which triggered many of them to leave on their own. I had to fire a few who refused to work hard, and then I hired a new team and instilled new values and attitudes. Not everyone liked my tactics, of course, but it worked. To my surprise, the president of the company called me one day to congratulate me and ask how I was doing it. He expressed some concern over what he considered extreme measures, but he liked the results!

When you became a Christian, you came under new ownership. The apostle Paul said, "You are not your own; you were bought at a price" (1 Corinthians 6:19-20). That might mean some drastic changes, getting rid of old behaviors and ways of thinking; bringing in new ways of living. Out with the old values and attitudes; in with the new.

I like the way author and musician John Fischer discussed this new ownership:

> What does it mean to not belong to myself? I can think of a few things. It means that I should probably do a lot of consulting with my new owner. There is more to consider than just me and what I want to do; there is God and what He wants me to do. ... But in all instances it is the attitude of the heart that is most important. It is a submissive attitude toward God that He is looking for—what the Old Testament calls a broken and contrite heart. It's being always open and teachable because I realize my new owner has a different way of looking at things than what comes natural for me. In fact, over time I begin to realize what comes natural for me is often my biggest problem.[5]

This is one of the best things I've learned in life—and certainly one of the hardest to learn: *It's not about me. It's all about him.* But, like Adam and Eve, I so easily forget that fact and, again and again, act for myself.

Henry and Richard Blackaby said, "The fact that God can bring character development and personal growth out of any situation is conditional on people's willingness to submit to God's will. God is sovereign over every life, but those who yield their will to him will be shaped according to his purposes."[6]

As a spiritual seeker years ago when I was in my mid-twenties, the little booklets produced by Campus Crusade had a profound impact on my life. My niece, Julie, used *The Four Spiritual Laws* to introduce me to a relationship with Jesus as my Savior. A little later, I came across, *Would You Like to Know God Personally?* which helped me to more fully know Jesus as my Lord. Three little circles in that booklet challenged my viewpoint on life. And they still do.[7]

Life to the full can only be lived in the third circle. Leading a small group should only be done in that circle, as well. I'm learning that living in the third circle is an everyday decision—a decision of the will. But that decision will certainly bring conflict. Like the stores

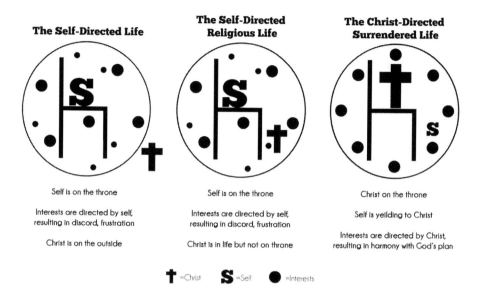

The Self-Directed Life

Self is on the throne

Interests are directed by self, resulting in discord, frustration

Christ is on the outside

The Self-Directed Religious Life

Self is on the throne

Interests are directed by self, resulting in discord, frustration

Christ is in life but not on throne

The Christ-Directed Surrendered Life

Christ on the throne

Self is yeilding to Christ

Interests are directed by Christ, resulting in harmony with God's plan

✝ =Christ   **S** =Self   ● =Interests

I turned around, the change in management of your life will create battles. As Fischer put it, "It used to be just me. Now I have me and the Spirit and we may not always be in sync."

Even the World's Greatest Small Group Leader dealt with this conflict. Before he began his ministry, he battled it out with Satan in the desert. Of course, Jesus submitted to the Word of God and did not yield to Satan. Then, at the end of his earthly ministry, in the Garden of Gethsemane, Jesus again faced the conflict head-on. His response to his Father was, "Your will must be done, not mine" (Luke 22:42, *God's Word*).

The fact that Jesus battled this conflict—the fact that he even had to say, "not mine"—means that Jesus, as a human, had a will that sometimes was not the same as the Father's will. Their wills—like yours and mine—were not always in sync. I know that might sound sacrilegious, but it is biblical, and it helps me, at least, to know that Jesus dealt with the same temptations I do, yet did not sin (Hebrews 4:15).

You and I have the same spiritual power that was available to Jesus in that desert and in the garden. We have the power of his Spirit within us to help us fight this battle and not yield to sin.

You are under new management, and he wants you to live your new life to the full. But that's not all—you also have a new citizenship.

A CHANGE IN CITIZENSHIP

When you became a Christian, you took on a new citizenship. You no longer belong to this world. Your citizenship in now in the kingdom of heaven. Comparing non-Christians and Christians of his day, the apostle Paul commented, "Their mind is on earthly things. But our citizenship is in heaven" (Philippians 3:19-20). Being a citizen of heaven means a change in values and priorities—a change from the world's systems and standards to those of your new king. It means a change in rules. You now live by God's Word, not by the principles of the world.

No one sneaks across the border or bribes their way into citizenship in heaven. It is a free gift with many privileges and opportunities, and yet, once you're in, important responsibilities come with being a citizen of heaven. Make sure you count the cost!

Jesus is a perfect example of someone who lived as a citizen of heaven while in this world. He was not of this world (John 8:23; 17:14, 16), and he reminded his disciples that neither were they (15:19). Neither the religious leaders, the disciples, nor Pilate understood Jesus' true citizenship even though the kingdom of heaven was one of his favorite subjects to talk about. He told Pilate, "My kingdom is not of this world. ... My kingdom is from another place" (John 18:36).

You are called to live in this world and yet not be a citizen of it. Pastor, speaker, and writer Warren Wiersbe said, "Our sphere of life is not this earth, but heaven; and the things that attract us and excite us belong to heaven, not to earth."[8] You are called to live like Abraham, who "made his home in the promised land like a stranger in a foreign country. ... For he was looking forward to the city with foundations, whose architect and builder is God" (Hebrews 11:9-10).

Take a moment now to consider these tough questions, and perhaps discuss them with your small group:

- Do you live in this world like a foreigner or a native?

- Are you living your life in "tents," not putting down roots because you know this is not your home, or are you settled in?

- Are you living in comfort here or in hope for your future home?

Part of living as a citizen of heaven is surrendering your own desires so you can carry out the will of the King. But how do you know his will? The answer is clear, even if it is not easy: "Do not conform to the pattern of this world, but be transformed by the renewing of your mind. Then you will be able to test and approve what God's will is" (Romans 12:2). When you surrender the things the world offers, no longer conforming to its ways, and when you allow your mind to be changed into a new way of thinking—a kingdom mindset—then God shows you his will for your life.

Try this today. Use Romans 12:2 as an acid test for every decision you make, everything you do, whatever enters your mind, every emotion that you feel. Does your decision, thought, emotion or action cause you to conform to the world's ways or be transformed to God's ways? This will take full attention and strict discipline, but it will help you know and understand God's will.

What specific changes do you need to make to live as a citizen of heaven? Take time to reflect on each of the Bible passages in the table on the next page. What do you still need to surrender, and what are your new responsibilities?

One more thing in regard to your new citizenship. The King—the one who has made you a citizen of his kingdom—has given you a significant role. While you are here in this world, he wants you to represent him as his ambassador. He has given you the message about

Verse	Passage	Surrender	Responsibilities
Matthew 6:19-21, 33	Do not store up for yourselves treasures on earth, where moths and vermin destroy, and where thieves break in and steal. But store up for yourselves treasures in heaven, where moths and vermin do not destroy, and where thieves do not break in and steal. For where your treasure is, there your heart will be also. . . . But seek first his kingdom and his righteousness, and all these things will be given to you as well.		
Romans 7:4-6	So, my brothers and sisters, you also died to the law through the body of Christ, that you might belong to another, to him who was raised from the dead, in order that we might bear fruit for God. For when we were in the realm of the flesh, the sinful passions aroused by the law were at work in us, so that we bore fruit for death. But now, by dying to what once bound us, we have been released from the law so that we serve in the new way of the Spirit, and not in the old way of the written code.		
Ephesians 2:1-10	As for you, you were dead in your transgressions and sins, in which you used to live when you followed the ways of this world and of the ruler of the kingdom of the air, the spirit who is now at work in those who are disobedient. All of us also lived among them at one time, gratifying the cravings of our flesh and following its desires and thoughts. Like the rest, we were by nature deserving of wrath. But because of his great love for us, God, who is rich in mercy, made us alive with Christ even when we were dead in transgressions—it is by grace you have been saved. And God raised us up with Christ and seated us with him in the heavenly realms in Christ Jesus, in order that in the coming ages he might show the incomparable riches of his grace, expressed in his kindness to us in Christ Jesus. For we are God's handiwork, created in Christ Jesus to do good works, which God prepared in advance for us to do.		
Colossians 3:1-3	Since, then, you have been raised with Christ, set your hearts on things above, where Christ is, seated at the right hand of God. Set your minds on things above, not on earthly things. For you died, and your life is now hidden with Christ in God.		

this kingdom, and he wants you to tell everyone you know about it (see 2 Corinthians 5:16-21). And—take note—this is not optional if you are a citizen of heaven. I'll discuss this more in Chapter 4.

If you are surrendering your will, you're off to a good start! That decision inexplicably leads to the next one, to surrender your assignment.

SURRENDER YOUR ASSIGNMENT

God gives the assignment. Your job is to surrender to his will and purpose for your life.

If his will and purpose is for you to lead a small group, a church, or a movement, then lead diligently (Romans 12:8)!

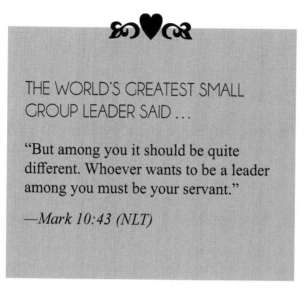

THE WORLD'S GREATEST SMALL GROUP LEADER SAID ...

"But among you it should be quite different. Whoever wants to be a leader among you must be your servant."

—*Mark 10:43 (NLT)*

If his will and purpose is for you to sweep floors, be a Christian lawyer, be a missionary to Iraq, or *fill in the blank*, then do it with all your heart, as serving the Lord, not men (Colossians 3:23).

When you took on a new citizenship, your way to the top changed drastically. Citizens of the world's system *aspire* to leadership. Citizens of heaven are *assigned* to leadership.

APPOINTED, NOT RECRUITED

Leading a small group (or anything else in the church) comes out of an assignment or appointment from God. This is critical and foundational to Christian leadership. When someone recruits you to a job that you are not called to, it's easy to throw in the towel when the going gets tough.

Are you a small group leader because someone recruited you, because there's a shortage of leaders, or because you have been called by God?

Let me be clear: You may have been recruited, even out of a sense of need, by someone in your church: a pastor, ministry point leader, coach, or the leader of your group, for instance. That does not mean you have not also been called. God often—actually, usually—uses other people as his ambassadors to call us into his service. You may have been primarily called as a small group host or facilitator, but now I'm talking to you about being a leader, and maybe you're thinking, Not so fast! I'm not a leader, just a host or facilitator.

Please let me encourage you.

First, don't underestimate yourself. The best leaders are often, at first, anyway, reluctant leaders. Humility is a vital trait of a godly leader.

Second, and I've said this before, it's not about you anyway! The best leaders are people who are simply willing to let God use them. God takes ordinary people and does extraordinary things through them.

Third, simply start where you are, in whatever role God has called you to, and be ready to grow into what God is making you into. Remember what Jesus told some guys who started as fishermen: "Follow me, and I will make you fishers of men!"

It comes down to this: You assume the role of a leader "not because you must, but because you are willing, as God wants you to be" (1 Peter 5:2). What's important is your willingness to let God use you as he wants for his kingdom work.

I think back about some of the policemen in New Orleans who started handing in their badges in the midst of the flooding and looting during and after Hurricane Katrina in 2005. I can understand why they'd want to quit under those horrific circumstances—I can't blame them, especially in a $16,000-a-year job. I'm guessing none of the officers who handed in their badges would have said they were "called" to their positions. Why? Because when you're called, you're willing to surrender—even your life.

52

This reminds me of an old story you may have heard: A pastor, a lawyer and an engineer were about to be guillotined. The pastor put his head on the block, they pulled the rope, and nothing happened. He said, "Praise God, I've been saved by divine intervention," and they let him go. The lawyer was then put on the block, and again the rope didn't release the blade. He said, "You can't try executing me a second time for the same crime," and he too was set free. The engineer was next, and they shoved his head into the guillotine. He looked up and quickly studied the release mechanism and said, "Hold on a second ... I see your problem." That's making a surrender for your calling!

Jesus warned his followers to count the cost of being his disciple. As a Christian leader, it's crucial to recognize Satan's strategy to weaken the church by attacking its leaders. The strategy is decapitation. Remove leadership, and affect the whole organization.

Being a small group leader is more than a commitment. Commitments are overrun by other commitments ... especially in our culture today. I remember well the line from an England Dan and John Ford Coley song: "Oh, it's sad to belong to someone else when the right one comes along." Unfortunately, that attitude is prevalent in today's world and in the church.

A commitment takes dedication. But a calling takes surrender. That reminds me of the lyrics of another song, one of my favorites, *For the Sake of the Call*: "I will abandon it all for the sake of the call." If God has called you to be a small group leader, say, "Yes, God. I will abandon it all for the sake of your call. I surrender."

That may not be easy. I remember when God called me and my wife to move to Idaho. Several relatives and friends could not comprehend how we could make the move. How could we move our kids away from their grandparents, aunts, uncles, and cousins, they asked. I admit it wasn't easy. It was tough. But we knew, and tried to explain to others, that God had called us to go. We felt like Abraham, who "obeyed and went," even though he did not know where he was going. Our calling by God trumped any possible circumstances, consequences, or even personal feelings.

UNEXPECTED CALLS

God often assigns leadership positions to unlikely people. He chose the shepherd boy, David, over his older, bigger, and more skilled brothers. He chose Jonah, even though he kept running away and hiding. He chose some ordinary and uneducated fishermen, tax collectors, and other assorted riffraff over the elite, educated Pharisees. Why? Because "the Lord does not look at the things man looks at. Man looks at the outward appearance, but the Lord looks at the heart" (1 Samuel 16:7). From those he chose in Scripture, I think one of the main attributes God looks at is a heart surrendered to him.

When Jesus called some fishermen, they surrendered their business, families, vocational identities, and who knows what else to follow him. When Jesus called Matthew, he surrendered his career. When he called Saul, he surrendered his religion, his reputation, and his retinal orientation. When he calls you, he is also looking for a surrendered heart.

YOU'RE GIFTED!

Spiritual leadership is a gift. You don't earn it. You can't achieve it. You don't really even deserve it. If you grab leadership, it's not a gift. You just accept it with a willing, surrendered heart. It's a gift of God's grace in your life.

Here's how the apostle Paul put it:

> By God's grace and mighty power, I have been given the privilege of serving him by spreading this Good News. Though I am the least deserving of all God's people, he graciously gave me the privilege of telling the Gentiles about the endless treasures available to them in Christ (Ephesians 3:7-8, NLT).

I've heard people say that only about 5-10 percent of the people in any given church have the spiritual gift of leadership. I wonder where they got that statistic. It's not in the Bible. I checked. I believe lots of God's people can be servant-leaders. And, by the way, that's the only kind of spiritual leader the Bible talks about.

God has and will give you the gift to lead as you need it. Like Moses, he'll put you into situations where you'll need to provide leadership. You may not think you have what it takes, but if he puts you in that situation, he'll also give you everything you need to carry out his will (see Exodus 4). He'll give it to you as a gift of his grace.

SURRENDER YOUR LEADERSHIP

Years ago, as a new Christian, I was thrust into ministry quickly. At the time I didn't understand surrender, so I tried to lead by my own power. I learned very quickly about God's power being made perfect in my weakness (2 Corinthians 12:9). I got really good at making God's power perfect! He used me even though I had no idea what I was doing most of the time. But I also made lots of mistakes.

GET OUT OF THE WAY SO GOD CAN GET TO WORK

I was sharing my faith—or trying to—with one couple in our apartment building. I spent months using every tactic I had learned, and then some, with no results. Finally, my wife told me to back off. I couldn't believe it. *What a backslider,* I thought. I was fulfilling the Great Commission, but I had married a heretic! Then she told me that perhaps I needed to leave room for the Holy Spirit to work in their lives. She was right, of course. I receded, and eventually the couple came to Christ—about a year after we moved from the building.

In my ministry, I've been in lots of overwhelming situations. I've spoken on the phone with people talking about committing suicide. I've walked into hospital rooms of dying patients surrounded by family members in need of comfort. I've entered homes where men have died in their prime. In one case—and I wasn't ready for this—the man's body was still on the floor in the living room when I walked in.

If I would have been faced with the same situations years ago, I may have done more damage than good by trying to minister in my own power. Over the years, however, I've learned more about surrender—yielding the situation completely to God. More and more I can respond as David did: "When I am overwhelmed, you alone know the way I should turn" (Psalm 142:3, NLT).

Now, as soon as I get a phone call or enter into a situation, the first thing I do is surrender the situation to God. I pray something such as this:

> God, you know I don't have whatever's needed to minister to this family. I don't have the right words, and I'm not sure how to handle this. I've got nothing! But I know that you do have all the right words and you do know what is needed. So I'm once again surrendering myself to you. Use me any way you want. If they need words, speak the words through my voice. If they just need someone to be there, help me to be quiet and to be there with them through this. If they need counsel, give me the words to say at the right time. Whatever their need, God, you know what it is, so use me anyway you want. I'm all yours.

I'm always amazed at what happens. God does his work, whether I understand it or not. There's nothing magical or mystical about it, but I know God has used my weakness to demonstrate his power. One family sent me a card that thanked me for how I ministered to them through my caring attitude, my words, and even my humor. When I received the letter I chuckled because I went into the situation with no idea how to handle it. But God did.

When you surrender your leadership to God, allowing him to use you any way he wants, you will minister in ways you thought you never could. In fact, you will learn, as I have, that it's not about what you do at all. As Mother Teresa so eloquently put it, "I am a little pencil in the hand of a writing God who is sending a love letter to the world."

WHAT SURRENDER REQUIRES

To learn to surrender, you first need to grow in some other biblical characteristics. The World's Greatest Small Group Leader illustrated all these character traits perfectly:

1. **Humility**—It all begins here. Surrender demands a humble heart. Jesus humbled himself when he "made himself nothing" and left heaven to become human (Philippians 2:7-8). Humility is the opposite of selfish ambition and vain conceit (v. 3).

2. **Authenticity**—A humble person can be who he or she is without pretenses. Even though he was, by his very nature, God (v. 6), Jesus came and lived as a man (v. 8). He never denied either part of his identity. He knew who he was.

3. **Vulnerability**—An authentic person can be open and honest with others; he has nothing to hide.

4. **Submission/Obedience**—A surrendered heart means you are submissive to authority. Jesus obeyed his Father in everything, even death (v. 8).

5. **Integrity**—All of these characteristics lead to integrity— uncompromising adherence to truth. Jesus was the model of integrity. He was the truth (John 14:6). Integrity elicits trust, a vital characteristic of a small group leader.

WHAT SURRENDER PRODUCES

A surrendered leader is one who is connected to the Vine. You are dependent on the Vine. You will produce much fruit (John 15:5). You naturally put the interests of others before your own by

- Listening to them

- Serving them

- Praying for them

- Loving them

These are some of the attributes of an effective leader, but one more needs further discussion.

SURRENDER PROPELS GROUP GROWTH

God has called you to help bring about spiritual growth in people's lives. But how does that happen, exactly? What's your role?

Imagine you are the captain of a sailboat. How do you make the vessel move forward toward your destination? The wind and only the wind supplies the power necessary for movement. If the wind is not blowing, you might as well forget raising the sails. How about having all the people on the boat blow as hard as they can into the sails? No, that won't work either. No matter how much effort you expend— no matter how much you huff and puff—you cannot move the ship forward. You cannot create wind.

So what do you do? You wait for the wind and then raise the sails to catch it. What happens if you do not raise the sails? Nothing. The power is accessible, but you must do your part in the partnership— raise the sails. The wind can only propel you forward when you are engaged in it. Sailing is a partnership between man and nature.

Spiritual growth is a collaborative effort between you and God. You cannot do it without God. He has ordained not to do it without you. The term for *Spirit* is the same for that of *wind* in both the Old and New Testaments. The Holy Spirit is the wind that provides the driving force of all spiritual growth. You cannot bring about spiritual growth in your own life or the lives of those you lead.

Neither are you a passive bystander. As the Holy Spirit moves, you must become engaged in that driving force. As a small group leader you have at least four vital sail-raising responsibilities:

1. Pray for the members of your group. That's your first and most important job.

2. Be an example to the flock. Let them see spiritual growth

happening in your own life by being involved in the spiritual disciples of worship, Bible reading, prayer, and others.

3. Involve the group every week in practices such as meeting in authentic community, studying and applying God's Word together, teaching and admonishing one another, praying together, serving together, and confessing your sins to each other.

4. Shepherd your members outside of group meeting times. Be prepared to mentor them in areas where they need to grow, as God leads you.

I'll tell you how to raise that last sail in much more detail in the next chapter.

TALK ABOUT IT

What specifically do you need to surrender to God right now?

Where do you need to stop leading so the Holy Spirit can lead?

What can you do to raise the sails to engage in what God wants to do through you?

TRAIT #3

Shepherd

"Be shepherds of God's flock" (1 Peter 5:2). Peter began his description of your role as a small group leader by assigning you the position of shepherd, or spiritual guide, for the group. In the last two chapters, I've shown you the foundational heart attitudes for small group leadership. You cannot shepherd people like the World's Greatest Small Group Leader unless you are seeking and surrendering.

God's Word is rich in its discussion about shepherding. Moses, David, and Amos served as shepherds, and all were influenced greatly by that role in their leadership. *Shepherd* is applied in Scripture to God, Jesus, kings and other leaders of the people, and ministers (not necessarily paid staff ministers).

According to the *Practical Word Studies in the New Testament*, the duties of shepherds, whether literally or spiritually, are:

- to feed the sheep, even if they have to gather them in their arms and carry them to the pasture

- to guide the sheep to the pasture and away from the rough places and precipices

- to seek and save sheep who get lost

- to protect the sheep; shepherds are even willing to sacrifice their lives for the sheep

- to restore sheep who return after going astray

- to reward sheep for obedience and faithfulness

- to keep sheep separate from the goats

For you to fully understand what it means to be a group's shepherd, I need to distinguish between your role as a shepherd of the flock under your care and Jesus' role as the Chief Shepherd.

THERE IS ONE TRUE SHEPHERD

I'm using the word *shepherd* in this book to describe your role as a small group leader. But that's not quite right. Let me explain:

God's church has lots of sheep, but only one true shepherd.

While Peter calls you a shepherd, it is essential to understand that you are not the Chief Shepherd. That role belongs exclusively to Jesus.

That God is our only shepherd is a theme throughout Scripture. King David declared it centuries earlier: "The Lord is my shepherd" (Psalm 23:1). His son Solomon also confirmed this: "The words of the wise prod us to live well. They're like nails hammered home, holding life together. They are given by God, the one Shepherd" (Ecclesiastes 12:11, *The Message*). The Lord is our only source of wisdom and our one true shepherd.

The *New Life Version* renders "Chief Shepherd" in 1 Peter 5 as "Head Shepherd." Just as Jesus is the head of the body of Christ (Ephesians 4:15; Colossians 1:18), he is the Head Shepherd. He is the real leader of "your" group.

Even the writers on Wikipedia recognize the significance of this:

The Great Shepherd is one of the thrusts of Biblical scripture. This illustration encompasses many ideas, including God's care for his people, His discipline to correct the wandering sheep, as well as the tendency of humans to put themselves into danger's way and their inability to guide and take care of themselves apart from the direct power and leading of God.

Jesus is the Head Shepherd of the group, yet God designed his church as a partnership with human beings. You are called to represent him, carry out his plans, fulfill his commission, and perform the ministry he gives you to do. He is the King; you are his ambassador. He is the owner of the group; you are his steward. He is the Chief Shepherd; you

THE WORLD'S GREATEST SMALL GROUP LEADER SAID . . .

"*I* am the good shepherd. I know *my* sheep," and *my* sheep know me. ... I have other sheep that are not of this sheep pen. I must bring them also. They too will listen to my voice, and there will be *one* flock and *one* shepherd."

—*John 10:14-16 (emphasis added)*

are his "subordinate shepherd." The table on the following page details some of the differences.

After Jesus rose from the dead, he called Peter as one of his first subordinate shepherds: "Feed my lambs ... take care of my sheep ... feed my sheep" (John 21:15-17). Whose lambs? Whose sheep? Not Peter's. Not yours. Not your senior minister's. Jesus'!

Jesus' Role as the Chief Shepherd	Your Role as a Subordinate Shepherd
• Knows his sheep and makes it possible for the sheep to know him • Lays down his life for the sheep • Calls the sheep by name • Seeks after the lost sheep and draws them to himself • Provides eternal life and abundant life	• Follow the Chief Shepherd • Model following the Chief Shepherd • Help the sheep under your care to hear and respond to the Chief Shepherd's voice • Guide the sheep under your care to follow the Good Shepherd and reach out to sheep without a shepherd • Encourage the sheep to live the abundant life

So let's review this vital spiritual leadership principle. Jesus is …

- The Good Shepherd (John 10:11, 15)

- The Great Shepherd (Hebrews 13:20-21)

- The Shepherd and Guardian of Our Souls (1 Peter 2:25)

- The Chief Shepherd (1 Peter 5:4)

I'll continue to use the term *shepherd* to describe your role (and *subordinate shepherd* when needed for clarity). Just remember that you shepherd under the Chief Shepherd's authority—which is why the previous chapter about surrender is so vital. You shepherd the group as an act of stewardship. The group is not yours, but God has entrusted you with them for now to care for and manage well. I'll discuss stewardship of the group in more detail in Chapter 6.

Whether you host, facilitate, or lead the group, remember, you are one of the sheep. Jesus is your shepherd. You are not above the other sheep. You have no right to lord your role over them, because you are not the Lord, either. Jesus has called you as his representative and as a good steward to care for the fellow sheep he's temporarily entrusted to you. So take your responsibility seriously.

Jesus used the imagery of shepherds and sheep as a parable or metaphor. Parables usually have one simple, straightforward meaning from which we can learn. But be careful not to read too much into them or stretch them beyond the intended application. For instance, in the real world of real sheepfolds and shepherds, sheep are not entrusted to lead other sheep or called as subordinate shepherds. But in the spiritual world, this is the case. We are more than just dumb sheep. Jesus calls each of us as his partners in his mission.

WE ARE SUBORDINATE SHEPHERDS

My friend and fellow pastor, Steve Idle, once described small group leaders like this: "I believe a Life Group Leader is one of the most significant ministry opportunities we offer at Northeast. Rarely does a person have the opportunity to impact the life of a fellow believer the way a Life Group Leader can."

That's a great summary of the identity, influence, and importance of shepherd-leaders in God's church. Unfortunately, over the years the church lost its biblical roots of shepherding. In many churches, the pastoral position has been assumed by one church employee who futilely attempts to shepherd up to 100 (and sometimes more) people. The Good Shepherd chose 12 for his group, and he spent even more of his time discipling three of them.

As a small group leader, you are given the authority and responsibility to carry out the pastoral ministry of the church in your group. That sounds like a big assignment, but you're not alone!

The World's Greatest Small Group Leader modeled shepherding for the members of his group and us. He illustrated how vitally important the role of a shepherd is as he walked among the throngs of people and "had compassion on them, because they were harassed and helpless, like sheep without a shepherd" (Matthew 9:36). That these people were aimlessly wandering through life with no one to guide, care for, feed, and protect them broke Jesus' heart. So take your assignment of shepherding seriously. You are an answer to his prayer for more workers to bring in the harvest (vv. 37-38).

As you grow into this role of a shepherd-leader …

- Do not view yourself merely as a Bible-study teacher or the equivalent of a Sunday school teacher who presents lessons to the group.

- Do not limit your role to planning and conducting discussions.

- Do not think of yourself only as a disc-jockey who puts the DVD in the player and pushes play.

Small group pioneer Ralph Neighbour put it this way:

> The Shepherd never says, "I will tend the flock on Wednesday evenings from 7:00 to 9:30 P.M." No! The Shepherd lives with the flock, sleeps in the fields with the flock, goes into treacherous situations to find a lost sheep, and carries the lambs in his arms. The Shepherd is the first one to go into the "valley of the shadow of death" to lead sheep to "green pastures."[9]

To try to get my point across about the difference between a good shepherd-leader as Dr. Neighbour describes, and one who is, well, not so good, I wrote this satirical (and a bit sarcastic) parody of Psalm 23:

The Psalm of the No-Good Shepherd

This leader is the shepherd
I do not want.
He maketh me sit down on green love seats;
he leadeth me to meetings.
He ignoreth my soul.
He leadeth me to complete my homework assignment—
It taketh three hours, for heaven's sake.
Yea, though I walk through the valley of downsizing and debt,

you are not with me.

Your wife and the church staff; they run from me.

You preparest a table of fattening foods before me.

You are my enemies.

My blood's about to boil;

My disappointment overflows.

Surely your incessant e-mails and texts will follow me all the days of my life;

And I shall dwell in this lousy group forever!

The Bible is not silent about your role as a small group shepherd. Look at the following scriptural guidelines based on John 10:1-16:

The Difference Between a Shepherd and a Hired Hand	
SHEPHERD	HIRED HAND
• Cares to the point of sacrifice	• Quits when the going gets tough
• Knows sheep personally	• Knows the sheep as a flock
• Intimate relationship with God	• Is in it for personal advancement
• Heart for the sheep	• Just doing the job
• Provides eternal life and abundant life	• Encourage the sheep to live the abundant life

Here are a few more of the significant shepherding passages from God's Word:

"Keep watch over yourselves and all the flock of which the Holy Spirit has made you overseers. Be shepherds of the church of God, which he bought with his own blood" (Acts 20:28).

"Be sure you know the condition of your flocks, give careful attention to your herds" (Proverbs 27:23).

THE MAJOR ROLES OF A SHEPHERD LEADER

As I mentioned earlier, you can divide your shepherding role into three vital relationships: connecting your group into authentic community with one another, discipling them to grow in their relationship with God, and encouraging them to make an impact by serving others. I'll address each of these throughout the rest of this chapter.

#1: Guide Them to Authentic Community

One of the first things you do as a leader is build relationships with the members of the group. This should begin way before the first meeting.

Finding Your Group

If you are just getting started and do not have group members yet, start with prayer. Ask God to show you exactly who he wants in your group. Then keep your eyes open to whom he will send. It's highly likely—but not absolute—that these will be people already in your circle, people you already know. They may be friends, neighbors, co-workers, people you serve with or otherwise know from church, for instance.

To keep your eyes open for whom God sends, ask him for the spiritual eyes to see. In John 1:47-49, when Jesus saw Nathanael approaching him, he said, "Here is a true Israelite, in whom there is nothing false." This surprised Nathanael: "How do you know me?" he asked. Jesus answered, "I saw you while you were still under the fig tree before Philip called you." How did Jesus "see" Nathanael, whom he had never met? He had been praying that the Father would make known to him those whom the Father was going to give him out of the world (John 17:6).

Several years ago, I started a new "turbo group" (a small group that lasts about three to twenty-four months in which every member is a leader-in-training and will begin a new group at the conclusion of the group). When I first began planning it, I knew that the selection of this group would be critical to the future of our small group ministry. So I decided not to "recruit" the group or even make a list of names. Instead, I prayed every day that God would bring them. Because I believed these would be future leaders in our small group ministry, I did what the World's Greatest Small Group Leader said to do: "Ask the Lord of the harvest, therefore, to send out workers into his harvest field" (Matthew 9:38). I also asked for God to give me the eyes to see them when they came.

Larry walked in the front door of our office building one day and asked to see the small group minister. I reluctantly set aside my turbo group planning and went out to meet him, a bit dismayed by the unannounced intrusion into my work—I thought the visitor was a salesperson. I soon discovered that Larry and his wife Glenda had been led to Christ by Ralph Neighbour, one of the pioneers of small group ministry. Larry and Glenda had spent years in ministry themselves, and had recently moved to Louisville, looking for a church where they could be involved. Larry wanted to get back to his passion for discipleship in small groups.

I had known Chris and Tiffany for several years. Chris works on our backstage crew and has a huge servant's heart. I saw Chris standing around one Sunday morning before the service. It seemed odd to me that he apparently had nothing to do. Something inside me told me to go over and talk to him. I obeyed, but had no idea why. On my walk over, God told me—and it was extremely clear—to ask Chris to be in the group. I stopped for a moment in the middle of our lobby. Chris is a successful home builder in our area, but I had not yet considered him as a potential small group leader. Finally, I obeyed, told Chris about the group, and invited him. I expected him to say he'd have to think about it, but he immediately said, "Yeah! I'm in!" He went on to tell me that he and Tiffany had just talked and then prayed about getting into a small group the night before.

The stories about how each of the other members came and how I knew them are also unique and amazing. Each one is a testimony to the fact that God is the Chief Shepherd and the Lord of the Harvest!

Getting Started

As you begin, always start with a core group. One of the essential values of leading a small group is *Don't Start Alone!*

Meet together over meals, and build your team by getting to know one another. Begin planning the group together to develop ownership and involvement. Divide group tasks based on individuals' spiritual gifts and interests. Then, as a team, begin inviting others to your new group. (I'll discuss more about building a team with your group in Chapter 5.)

#2: Establish Relationships

The World's Greatest Small Group Leader integrated followers into his life rather than making them an extra appointment on an already crowded schedule. He called his group members "friends."

One of your primary tasks—if you can call it that—is to build relationships with group members. By starting with a core team, you have already begun. Now, as a team, each of you focuses on building relationships with other participants outside of meeting times.

God created people with a high need for real relationships. I read about a man who walked into a convenience store, threatened the clerk with a knife and demanded cash. When she gave him the money, he thanked her, walked out and sat down on the curb in front of the store. When police arrived, he jumped up and announced that he was the man they were looking for. The baffled police put him in cuffs and took him in.

At the trial, he gave his reason for robbing the store and immediately giving himself up: He had recently been released from jail, missed his cell mates, and wanted to return to jail to be with them. He got his wish.

That's the power of community. Some people will do just about anything for it. Paul and Silas could have related to this story:

> They were severely beaten, and then they were thrown into prison. The jailer was ordered to make sure they didn't escape. So the jailer put them into the inner dungeon and clamped their feet in the stocks. Around midnight Paul and

Silas were praying and singing hymns to God, and the other prisoners were listening (Acts 16:23-25, NLT).

You have probably figured out by now that the power of community increases the more people are together. Once a week or every other week meetings do not bring the kind of close-knit community you often see in the New Testament church. Take a look at a few verses that show how we are to engage in real community (not just meetings):

"Every day they continued to meet together" (Acts 2:46).

"Encourage one another daily" (Hebrews 3:13).

"Let us not give up meeting together, as some are in the habit of doing, but let us encourage one another" (Hebrews 10:25).

But how do you make this happen, short of incarcerating your whole group? It takes time together, spontaneous and planned. It may take proximity, meeting with the people where you live or work, for instance. It may take forming your group around people who have things in common. Instead of trying to find another brand new group of friends, ask yourself, Who is already in my life?

A big part of your role as a leader is to (1) live this kind of interdependent life yourself and (2) do everything you can to help develop this kind of authentic, ground-breaking community! As a shepherd, what do you do to make this happen?

- Pray regularly for and with the members of your group.

- Keep in touch between meetings. Call, email, visit.

- Accept everyone, regardless of personality differences. Author John Ortberg makes this astute observation: "[Here's] a deep theological truth: Everybody's weird. Every one of us—all we like sheep—have habits we can't control, past deeds we can't undo, flaws we can't correct."[10]

- Deal with conflicts up front. Don't try to wish them away or pretend they aren't there. For more help on this subject, see Pat Sikora's book, *Why Didn't You Warn Me?* (www. whydidntyouwarnme.com).

- Stay positive. Group members sometimes tend to become negative—about other people, the church, you name it. Turn the tide as soon as you can. It seems like a lot of people complain and gossip, but very few people want to be in a negative group.

- Focus on people, not the program. As Ralph Neighbour says, "The people in your group are the agenda!" [11]

Community is the environment in which everything else happens in a small group. It is the soil in which people grow spiritually.

#3: Guide Them to Grow Spiritually

As a small group shepherd you are in the most strategic position in the church to effect real, lasting life change and spiritual growth. The church's best method for caring, shepherding, loving, and growing people is you!

You may have heard assertions like this before, and while they are true, you may be asking how you are supposed to make it happen.

First, as a shepherd leader, be concerned for where people are in their spiritual journeys. You need to know where people are in order to shepherd them to where they ought to be. Accept group members where they are on their spiritual journeys. Treat each person with grace, not judgment. At the same time, help group members grow. Encourage, spur each other on, teach, and admonish one another in all wisdom.

Second, model a disciple's lifestyle. Spiritual growth must be happening in your life as the leader. You are a model for what life change looks like to others.

Third, keep providing the context. Continue to draw the group into increasing levels of authentic community. Don't give up meeting together, and people will grow.

Fourth, assess where group members are on their spiritual journeys.
While a number of spiritual assessments are available and beneficial,
using these tools is not a substitute for knowing the people in your
group and personally guiding them to grow. Like the Good Shepherd,
the best way for you to make assessments is to know your sheep.

Fifth, provide a process for growth to happen. Do application-
oriented Bible study as a group. Don't just study the Bible. Do what
it says! What do you study? The answer comes from knowing your
group and what they need most to grow. Ask a small group coach or
minister from your church for more help.

Sixth, be a spiritual parent to the group. Mentor some members one-
on-one. Ask group members who are relatively strong in one spiritual
area to disciple a person who would like to grow in that same area.
This involves everyone in the spiritual growth process.

Spiritual parenting means you don't see all group members the same.
You shepherd them individually because they are at different places
in their spiritual journeys. Some are infants, some are adolescents or
teens, while others are maturing adults.

The apostle John wrote in 1 John 2:12-14:

> I write to you, dear children,
>> because your sins have been forgiven on account of
>> his name.
> I write to you, fathers,
>> because you have known him who is from the beginning.
> I write to you, young men,
>> because you have overcome the evil one.
> I write to you, dear children,
>> because you have known the Father.
> I write to you, fathers,
>> because you have known him who is from the beginning.
> I write to you, young men,
>> because you are strong,
>> and the word of God lives in you,
>> and you have overcome the evil one.

John had learned from his small group leader how to shepherd the sheep individually.

Finally, develop leaders. I'll discuss this more in Chapter 5, but it's important to mention it here because it's a part of every group member's spiritual growth process. Continually developing and deploying new leaders is essential for what comes next.

#4: Guide Them to Where the Chief Shepherd Wants Them to Go

Here's a fact borne from years of experience: Group members do not always want to go where they need to go. They resist growing spiritually, being open to new people, stepping out to serve others, stepping up to become leaders, and sending out members to birth new groups. Group members sometimes prefer comfort to counting the cost.

From what I understand, sheep can be pretty stubborn animals. My black lab can be pretty dogged, as well. She loves to go on car rides, so, if we're not careful, she'll jump in the van with the family even when she's not invited. She's usually a very good, obedient dog, but not when it comes to getting her out of that van!

I've had small group members who were the same way. Once you get them into a group, they never want to leave! Jesus says, Go and make disciples, but it does not matter. All they want to do is stay and go for a ride!

Your role as a small group shepherd-leader is to take group members where they do not always want to go—to the places where the Chief Shepherd is commanding you to go. That may not always be easy and definitely not comfortable, but it's one of your most important responsibilities. Your job is to listen to the Chief Shepherd's voice closely, every day. Read his Word regularly. Stay involved in learning and growing yourself. Continue to be equipped for your role as a small group leader. Go to every training event and read every book you can (www.SmallGroupLeadership.com provides lots of help for shepherd-leaders).

I've seen many groups—and even entire churches—kowtow to members who prefer comfort rather than following God's commands. I've heard small group ministers say something like, "Well, our members won't open up their groups to new members or send out members to start groups, so we've changed our methodology to make it work with what we can reasonably expect our groups to do."

May I implore you? Don't do this! Hold high the values that the World's Greatest Small Group Leader gave us. His commission is to go and make disciples ... so go and make disciples!

And don't ever forget that your sheep have an enemy out there who is ready to deceive, diminish, and devour them. Peter reminded his readers—and us, "Be self-controlled and alert. Your enemy the devil prowls around like a roaring lion looking for someone to devour" (1 Peter 5:8).

As your group is going into the world, your job is to help guard members against attacks. Of course, you can't do this on your own, but only by God's mighty power. The shepherd David reported that "When a lion or a bear came and carried off a sheep from the flock, I went after it, struck it and rescued the sheep from its mouth. When it turned on me, I seized it by its hair, struck it and killed it" (1 Samuel 17:34-35). That's impressive shepherding! But look at how he did it; he said it was the Lord "who delivered me from the paw of the lion and the paw of the bear" (v. 37).

You will not be fighting lions and bears, but you are on a dangerous and crucial mission. The last thing the enemy wants is for your group to grow spiritually. He knows that Christ followers who are transformed into Christ's likeness (2 Corinthians 3:18) become dangerous to his agenda. So he will put up a fight, and he'll start with you.

Perhaps you've never considered leading your small group as doing spiritual battle, but it is a more real and critical fight than any battle ever fought in this physical world. So start your preparation on your knees. Pray through Ephesians 6:10-20. Pray specifically for each member of your group. Surrender yourself to God. Commit your plans to him. Submit to his authority and power. Acknowledge that it is his group, not yours. Ask him for his protection as you lead your group where the Chief Shepherd is calling you to go.

The World's Greatest Small Group Leader said, "I'm here to invite outsiders, not coddle insiders" (Matthew 9:13, *The Message*). That's what he's put you here for, too. I'll talk more about it in Chapter 4.

TALK ABOUT IT

Take a moment now to write down two specific things you will do differently to shepherd your group more like the Good Shepherd.

1. _____

2. _____

TRAIT #4
Serve

I'm a huge college basketball fan. During March Madness every year, I'm usually glued to the television, following the tournaments. I love watching the games, of course, but I also like some of the commercials. In one, years ago, Coach K (Mike Krzyzewski, head coach of Duke) made a fascinating comment: "I don't see myself as a basketball coach. I see myself as a leader who happens to coach basketball." That's interesting, but it's backwards for Christian leaders. Jesus calls us to see ourselves not so much as leaders but as servants who happen to lead.

Did you know that your very nature as a Christian is to be a servant? When God bought you with Jesus' blood (Ephesians 1:7) and you surrendered your life to him, you became his servant. You belong to him (Romans 14:8).

Jesus spent a lot of time trying to teach his small group this lesson. It took them a long time and a lot of bickering about who was greatest before they got it. In fact, it was not until after Jesus performed the ultimate act of service that they understood fully and began to live with servant attitudes.

Jesus and the apostle Paul spent a lot of time and effort trying to convince believers of their identity as God's servants—not servants of other things:

Passage	Scripture (NLT)	Serve God, Not :
Matthew 6:24	No one can serve two masters. For you will hate one and love the other; you will be devoted to one and despise the other. You cannot serve both God and money.	Money
Romans 6:6	Our old sinful selves were crucified with Christ so that sin might lose its power in our lives. We are no longer slaves to sin.	Sin
Romans 7:6	Now we can serve God, not in the old way by obeying the letter of the law, but in the new way of living in the Spirit.	The Law
Romans 16:18	Such people are not serving Christ our Lord; they are serving their own personal interests.	Yourself
Galatians 4:8	Before you Gentiles knew God, you were slaves to so-called gods that do not even exist.	Idols
Colossians 3:23-24	Work willingly at whatever you do, as though you were working for the Lord rather than for people. Remember that the Lord will give you an inheritance as your reward, and that the Master you are serving is Christ.	People

Like the World's Greatest Small Group Leader, your spiritual nature is to be a servant (Philippians 2:7). And, like Jesus, your role as a leader is to model servanthood to others. So, "never be lacking in zeal, but

80

keep your spiritual fervor, serving the Lord" (Rom. 12:11). Or as the *New Living Translation* puts it, "serve the Lord enthusiastically." In our main passage from 1 Peter 5:2-4, Peter says we are to be "eager to serve." Are you eager and enthusiastic to serve? That's our calling as spiritual leaders.

A SERVANT WHO LEADS

Your nature is to serve. God calls some servants to lead. It's never the other way around. If you can serve best by leading, and that is what God has called you to, then, by all means, lead—with diligence! (Romans 12:8). But if you can serve better in some other fashion, or if someone else can lead better than you, or if God has not called you to lead, then serve in some other way—with diligence!

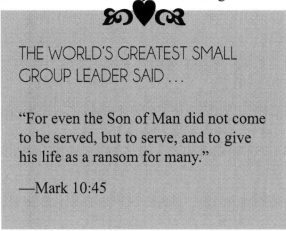

THE WORLD'S GREATEST SMALL GROUP LEADER SAID . . .

"For even the Son of Man did not come to be served, but to serve, and to give his life as a ransom for many."

—Mark 10:45

How you approach leadership—as a leader first or as a servant first—makes all the difference in the world. If you come at leadership as a leader first, you naturally try to control, make decisions, push your agenda, and give orders. If you come at leadership as a servant first, you build partnerships and shared leadership. You develop a team. Leadership is not a power play or an ego trip for you. You serve in this role because you are called to it, because people need a shepherd.

As a servant leader you will discover the need to fight the stature of the position. You live it with humility. Servant-leaders are often somewhat reluctant to lead, not because they don't think they can or doubt God's call, but because of the stature our society often assigns to leaders.

The Difference Between Leader-First and Servant-First Leadership[12]	
LEADERS FIRST …	SERVANTS FIRST …
• Naturally try to control, make decisions, and give orders	• Assume leadership only if it is the best way to serve
• Are "driven" to lead	• Are "called" to lead
• Are possessive about their leadership position; they think they "own" it	• View leadership as an act of stewardship. If someone else is a better leader, they will partner with the person or find another place to serve
• Dislike feedback; it is threatening to their position	
	• Like feedback; it helps them serve better

SERVE YOUR GROUP

While your primary call is to serve God, not man, you are empowered, enabled, and entrusted as his subordinate shepherd to serve your group. You serve God by serving others. Quite simply, you lead your group to "serve one another in love" (Galatians 5:13).

Serve your group eagerly and enthusiastically. That takes GUTS!

Genuinely: "Love each other with genuine affection, and take delight in honoring each other." (Romans 12:10, NLT).

Unconditionally: God's love for us doesn't depend on what we do. It's unconditional. In biblical community we accept and love one another "as is" no matter what. They don't have to earn it.

Tangibly: In deed, not just words. "Let us think of ways to motivate one another to acts of love and good works" (Hebrews 10:24, NLT).

Sacrificially: Jesus said, "There is no greater love than to lay down one's life for one's friends" (John 15:13, NLT).

How can you serve your group members "tangibly" (as well as genuinely, unconditionally, and sacrificially)? Here are a few ideas.

- Make them dinner with all the trimmings

- Watch their kids and arrange for a night out on the town

- Take them to, or pick them up from, the airport—no matter what time it is

- Wash their vehicles

- Help with a household project

- Go to their kids' games and cheer

- Mow their lawn

- Take an individual out for coffee and really listen

- Discover needs and meet them

- Ask them individually how you can pray for them—and then lift up their needs daily to God. Follow up by asking how things are going.

THE WORLD'S GREATEST SMALL GROUP LEADER SAID . . .

"Those who are the greatest among you should take the lowest rank, and the leader should be like a servant."

—*Luke 22:26, NLT*

SERVE TOGETHER AS FRIENDS

After Jesus had spent nearly three years with his small group, he brought them together for a going away party. He was preparing to go away, but first he had to prepare them. He began by modeling for them how to serve one another by washing their feet. They shared a meal together, and he taught them some valuable lessons:

> I'm no longer calling you servants because servants don't understand what their master is thinking and planning. No, I've named you friends because I've let you in on everything I've heard from the Father. You didn't choose me, remember; I chose you, and put you in the world to bear fruit, fruit that won't spoil. As fruit bearers, whatever you ask the Father in relation to me, he gives you. But remember the root command: Love one another (John 15:15-17, *The Message*).

I see several vital principles in this passage for any group:

1. **You serve as friends.** This may seem obvious, but it wasn't to Jesus' group. It must have been a big deal to them that Jesus called them his friends. He was their Rabbi—their teacher—and they were his disciples. Now he was saying, "I'm calling you my equals, my friends." They were in authentic community with one another. Even though Jesus was their Lord and Teacher, they were now all co-laborers in the Father's kingdom. They had been serving together—side-by-side—for a couple years. Now Jesus wanted them to continue serving together as friends, knowing that he would continue to be with them in spirit.

   Like that group, yours is a group of friends who are called to serve together. The Chief Shepherd is still here to guide you as you go into the world to serve.

2. **Remember that Jesus has chosen you as a leader, not the other way around.** The significance is that since he chose you to lead, your responsibility is to do what he calls you to do. If you had chosen him, you might still think you're in charge, making all the decisions. Your nature as a Christian is to serve God. He'll tell you what to do.

3. **He expects you to bear fruit.** He did not put you in the position of a small group leader to make sure the group is comfortable, to just

do Bible study, or to just have great fellowship. Your job is to bear fruit, fruit that will last.

4. **Don't forget—love one another!** That's the root command behind everything you do. Love each other in your group—and then extend that love to others outside your group. Let the love that God is pouring into you overflow into the lives of people around you.

An overriding principle of this passage is this: The group does not exist primarily for its members; it exists for others.

One morning on the Christian radio station I usually listen to, a local pastor of the "church of the week" talked about the nature of the church. He said the teens from his congregation had written essays about the church, and all of them used the word *safe* in their descriptions. The pastor went on to say that this is an accurate portrayal of the church.

What do you think? Does *safe* describe the heart of Christ's church?

Safe or Dangerous?

Perhaps it's a matter of perspective. We do want people to feel like the church, and every small group within it, is a safe place. They will be accepted for who they are and where they are in life. They will not be attacked or abused.

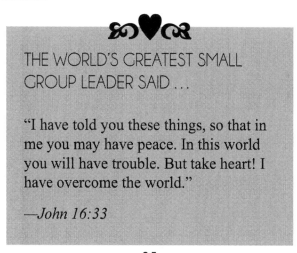

THE WORLD'S GREATEST SMALL
GROUP LEADER SAID ...

"I have told you these things, so that in me you may have peace. In this world you will have trouble. But take heart! I have overcome the world."

—*John 16:33*

On the other hand, God's Word portrays a church that is dangerous. It's in a war for the eternal destinies of humankind. It's a place of surrender and sacrifice. Peace comes in the midst of all this, as we put our trust in Christ. We are eternally safe because of his suffering, but we are on the front lines of a battle every day.

I think that is the gist of what Jesus was trying to teach his followers in Matthew 10, when he sent out the twelve to do ministry. He told them, "Do not suppose that I have come to bring peace to the earth. I did not come to bring peace, but a sword" (Matthew 10:34).

That does not sound very safe to me! It has always fascinated me that in this passage Jesus says he did not come to bring peace, and yet he is the Prince of Peace. He said, "Peace I leave with you; my peace I give you. I do not give to you as the world gives. Do not let your hearts be troubled and do not be afraid" (John 14:27).

Perhaps Jesus words in John 14:27 hold the secret for great small groups. The world defines peace as safety from trouble, but Christians know that in this world there *will* be trouble. Jesus has overcome the world, however. While difficulties and hardships will come, we do not have to let our hearts be troubled. As Christians, we do not need to seek safety and comfort. That is not the purpose of Christ-centered, kingdom-minded small groups. We seek the mind of Christ—his purpose, will, and peace in the midst of whatever may come our way.

As Christians, we have peace because we have Christ. He gives us life to the full in the midst of troubles.

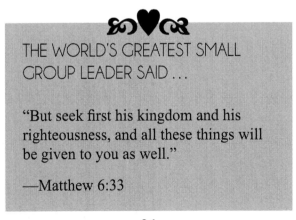

THE WORLD'S GREATEST SMALL GROUP LEADER SAID . . .

"But seek first his kingdom and his righteousness, and all these things will be given to you as well."

—Matthew 6:33

What You Can Do

One of your responsibilities as a small group leader is to keep a compelling vision in front of the group. Remind and encourage members that when you are involved in Jesus' mission and ministry, you will face trouble along the way. Ministry is not safe, but Jesus will provide his peace, comfort, and eternal safety as you carry out his commission. Here are five things you can do as a leader:

- Remind group members frequently of your mission and group purposes. Use God's Word to teach the group about God's calling on the lives of Christians.

- Pray together with the same kind of power and vision with which the early church prayed (e.g. Acts 4:23-31).

- Build a community that cares deeply for one another: "All the believers were one in heart and mind. No one claimed that any of his possessions was his own, but they shared everything they had" (Acts 4:32).

- Equip group members for acts of service. Ephesians 4:11-13 was written not just for paid church staff members. It's written to you as a leader and shepherd as well. It calls you to "prepare God's people for works of service."

- Build a community that boldly reaches out to the world. "With great power the apostles continued to testify to the resurrection of the Lord Jesus, and much grace was upon them all" (Acts 4:33).

- Find ways to lovingly serve your community.

Getting out of your La-Z-Boys™ and loveseats and into the world may be a different paradigm for your group. It may scare some. It may sound terribly dangerous. Some group members may waver or even fight you on this. As a leader, stand firm. Have compassion for your group and those who have no Shepherd.

THE WORLD'S GREATEST SMALL
GROUP LEADER SAID ...

"You are the light of the world. A town
built on a hill cannot be hidden. Neither
do people light a lamp and put it under
a bowl. Instead they put it on its stand,
and it gives light to everyone in the
house. In the same way, let your light
shine before others, that they may see
your good deeds and glorify your Father
in heaven."

—*Matthew 5:14-16*

The church where I serve has become known in Louisville as the
#LovetheVille church (we use that hashtag on everything; it has
become a big part of our vision and identity). We serve our community
primarily through our small groups. It's much better to serve together
than alone. Serving also assures that our groups are not becoming
ingrown cliques.

Your church and community have tons of opportunities to serve. First,
you can serve together *inside* the church. Here are a few ideas that you
could do together as a group. Ask around for more:

- Campus cleanup or landscaping

- Take communion to shut-ins

- Work in the nursery or other area together (Group members may
  need to be approved and have background checks first. If so,
  volunteer to pay for the background checks.)

- Greet or usher

- Get a bunch of umbrellas and, on rainy days, walk people in from their cars

Some of these you could do on a rotating basis, say, the first Sunday of every month. Perhaps you could work with other groups to cover all the Sundays!

You can also do *externally focused* ministry. Our groups regularly serve together in a variety of places throughout our community. We encourage our groups to eventually adopt a ministry as their "community cause." They take the lead, planning and performing the ministry tasks together. In some cases, they have joined together with an existing ministry to regularly help them. In other cases, our groups have formed their own ministries and community causes.

Several years ago, one group adopted a military helicopter pilot in Iraq. They regularly helped the family and sent care packages to the soldier. They even joined the pilot in ministering to the children of Iraq by sending candy that the helicopters dropped as "candy bombs" to the children. The candy bombs helped the children to not be afraid of the U.S. helicopters. This group's ministry to one family is having an impact in the world!

Another group began making peanut-butter-and-jelly sandwiches and putting them in sacks with apples and other snacks. They delivered the lunches to many homeless people in downtown Louisville. Later, other groups joined them and it finally grew into a church-wide ministry.

I could tell you about many more of these "small" group ministries that are not small at all! These are not ordinary, safe and comfortable small groups. They are mission-minded, serving groups that are making a big impact for Christ in our community. When your group moves out of the safe and comfortable and serves your community, you model authentic, profoundly powerful community to the world.

GO AND TELL TOGETHER

The World's Greatest Small Group Leader asked a philosophical question: "Who needs a doctor: the healthy or the sick?" The answer seems obvious, but the implication to your small group is more profound. Jesus then revealed his life mission: "I'm here to invite outsiders, not coddle insiders" (Matthew 9:13, *The Message*).

Your small group exists for the same purpose: to invite outsiders, not coddle insiders! Your group is a community with a cause.

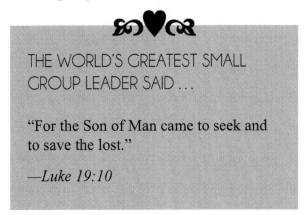

THE WORLD'S GREATEST SMALL
GROUP LEADER SAID . . .

"For the Son of Man came to seek and to save the lost."

—Luke 19:10

Community-Based Invitations

The apostle John made a riveting connection between community and reaching out to our world in 1 John 1:3: "We proclaim to you what we have seen and heard, so that you also may have fellowship with us. And our fellowship is with the Father and with his Son, Jesus Christ."

For many years, the church has taught an "individualistic invitational style" of evangelism: You, as an individual, go out and share your faith with another individual, and you invite that person to come into a "personal relationship with Jesus" (a phrase that isn't in the Bible).

The Bible teaches a community-based invitational style. A community of believers ("we") invite people into our fellowship (John's use of *our fellowship* is important; it indicates not just any kind of fellowship, but fellowship that was distinguishingly Christian)—a fellowship with the Father and his Son at its center.

The implications are:

• You, as a Christian, are in Christ-centered community.

- You invite others who are not in that community.

- When people come, they have the opportunity to join not only in your community, but, by its essence, into communion with God.

Bridge-Building, Bridge-Crossing Groups

Christians have used the "bridge illustration" for years to share their faith. My niece Julie used it effectively to lead me to Jesus. Leaders used to draw in community or small groups on the right side of the illustration, representing that once you have crossed the bridge you should get into fellowship with other Christians.

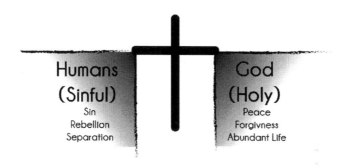

That worked to a large extent years ago, when most Americans were relatively close to the left side of the gap. Christianity was still the dominant faith in the country, it had a relatively good reputation, and people were fairly accepting of it. It didn't take much to move people toward the bridge.

Today, however, the bridge is miles away from many Americans. It is obscured by negativity about Christianity and the church and many other large cultural and societal barriers.

That's why the new science (it's actually not new at all!) is to place small group community on the left side of the illustration. Your small group can meet people where they are, serve them, and invite them into your community with a cause. Then you can walk with them together through the various pits and obstacles to the bridge. Bill Hybels, senior pastor at Willow Creek Community Church in South Barrington, Illinois, has said that believers have two gifts to give to the world. One is Jesus (John 3:16) and the other is our community.

THE PROFOUND POWER OF COMMUNITY

The apostle John wrote down Jesus' words in what I think is the most amazing passage about community in the Bible: John 17:20-26. This passage shows the profound power of authentic community.

- Jesus was praying for you and me here: "My prayer is not for them alone. I pray also for those who will believe in me through their message" (v. 20). He was praying for one simple and yet extraordinary thing, that we may be one ... just as he and the Father are one! His deep desire for us is to experience the kind of community that the Godhead experiences.

- When we do relate to one another as Jesus and the Father—when we live in real, authentic community—we can have a huge impact on our world: "May they also be in us so that the world may believe that you have sent me" (v. 21). When we live in outward-focused community, the world will believe in Jesus.

In his commentary on this passage, Warren Wiersbe says,

> One of the things that most impresses the world is the way Christians love each other and live together in harmony. ... The lost world cannot see God, but they can see Christians; and what they see in us is what they will believe about God. If they see love and unity, they will believe that God is love. If they see hatred and division, they will reject the message of the Gospel.[13]

A COMMUNITY STRATEGY

Jesus has given us a strategy for reaching non-Christians in our world. It is repeated often throughout the gospels. It is, by its nature, an excellent small group strategy:

Come and see … Go and tell … Come and see … Go and tell …

The abundant life is not just about coming to Jesus; it's also about going and telling others about him. Your small group is much more than just a "come and see" group; it's also a "go and tell" group. So go and tell what you've seen and heard ... so that they can come into fellowship with you and see how good God really is!

HOW TO START GOING AND TELLING

How do you get started becoming a "go and tell" group? It all begins with you, the leader.

1. **You must go first and model it for your group members.** If they don't see your compassion for lost friends—if you don't even have any lost friends!—it's unlikely they will get excited about going and telling as a group.

2. **Make going and telling a lifestyle.** Evangelism is not a program; it's what flows from the heart of a Christian who truly loves God and loves people. As author Jim Petersen said in *Living Proof,* "This kind of evangelism can hardly be called an activity in which one engages on certain occasions. It is life. Living itself becomes evangelistic."[14]

3. **To do either of the first two, you must begin with prayer.**

    *   Pray that God will give you his heart for the lost sheep.

    *   Ask him for opportunities to go and tell.

    *   Ask him to open your eyes to the harvest.

    *   Begin praying for people in your circles of influence by name. Pray for their needs (you may need to ask). Ask God to draw them to himself.

The key factor is prayer. The apostle Paul said, "I pray that you may be active in sharing your faith, so that you will have a full understanding of every good thing we have in Christ" (Philemon 6). Years ago I came across the following quote that says it all: "Evangelism without intercession is like an explosive without a detonator. Intercession without evangelism is like a detonator without an explosive."[15]

God has given you the responsibility and opportunity as his ambassador to share what he has freely given you. And he will never leave you alone in the task.

Next, help the group begin going and telling. If this is new, take one level at a time.

Three Levels of Going and Telling in a Small Group [16]

Let's get even more specific and practical. Determine the readiness of your group to become a going and telling group. Begin at the appropriate level and then continue developing more and more of a missional mindset in your group:

LEVEL 1: Support One Another's Efforts

- Use icebreakers that get members talking about their non-Christian friends, neighbors, co-workers, and family members.

- Learn how to go and tell. Use any number of available studies on how to share your faith, go through a book together, or study Bible passages about sharing your faith.

- Make applications of your current study to going and telling.

- Pray.

LEVEL 2: Go Together to Plant Seeds

- Throw a "Matthew Party." This is a party, based on Matthew 9:9-13, to which you invite a few members of your small group and their non-Christian friends. Nothing particularly "spiritual" has to be planned. Just pray first and watch for what God does.

- Leverage people in the group with evangelism gifts. Perhaps hand off ownership of this group role to them. Maybe group members invite them along to meet a non-Christian friend. (Some have the spiritual gift of evangelism, but we're all called to go and tell.)

- Leverage church events strategically. As a group, discuss who you can invite. Pray together for the event beforehand.

- Leverage social events of members. To what events can group members invite their friends? Sports events? Art fairs? Car shows?

LEVEL 3: Invite Seekers to Your Group

- Use the "Empty Chair." Leave a chair open to symbolize the fact that you are open to new people joining you. Pray for the person(s) who will fill your empty chair.

- Use natural curriculum rhythms. Invite people to join you at the beginning of a new study so they are on the same page as the rest of the group. Purposely study a subject that non-Christian friends may be interested in considering (i.e. marriage, raising children, and finances).

- Remember, the leader must go first!

See Chapter 6 of my book, *Small Group Vital Signs*, for even more ideas on how to minister and be a witness to others.

One of my favorite scenes is a small group, one that has helped a friend cross the bridge, celebrating together as their friend is baptized. Sometimes it happens in a swimming pool or hot tub of a member's home. Sometimes it happens at the church building with one of the group members baptizing their friend.

Either way, it's a fulfillment of 1 John 1:3. The group has proclaimed to this person what they have seen and heard so their friend could have real fellowship with them. Now, this new Christian has fellowship not only with them, but with the Father and his Son, Jesus Christ. That is a reason to celebrate!

MORE THAN YOU CAN IMAGINE!

What are your plans for your small group? From my experience, if they were honest, many small group leaders would say something like, "To get through my lesson this week." Some groups may have plans through the current study, but few that I've seen have a one- or two-year plan. That's unfortunate, because research shows that goal setting is one of the main factors in helping small groups grow and multiply themselves.

Here's a great promise: "Put God in charge of your work, then what you've planned will take place" (Proverbs 16:3, *The Message*). *Small Group Vital Signs* includes a chapter, "A Healthy Group Has Proactive Leadership," that discusses in much more depth the vitality of goals and plans. One of the things we learned in our group evaluation (the basis for that book) was that a direct correlation exists between groups that have (written) goals and plans and groups that are healthy in all the other vital signs of a healthy group.

I want to close this chapter by encouraging you to plan. But don't just make a human-designed, human-sized plan; make a God-activated, God-sized plan for your group. A God-sized plan (GSP) should make you and your group members gasp and say, "No way can we do that!" (And that, of course, is the point.) It should drive your group members to their knees. It should be so big that if God isn't in it, it's destined to fail. In the corporate world, this is called a BHAG: a "Big Hairy Audacious Goal." (The BHAG concept comes from Christian business consultant and author Jim Collins in his book, *Good to Great*. See his web site at http://www.jimcollins.com.)

The World's Greatest Small Group Leader made God-sized plans. He had a three-year plan for his group: To turn a bunch of uneducated, ordinary, smelly fishermen into fishers of men—into the World's Greatest Small Group. And I believe wholeheartedly that what Jesus and his group did then, your group can do now!

Jesus' plan for his group was not only God-sized, it was also God-activated. Remember, Jesus did nothing except what the Father gave him to do.

Then Jesus gave his followers an even bigger, a seemingly impossible, God-sized plan: to go and make disciples of all nations. All nations! That's God-sized!

How will you determine your GSP? Do each of these yourself first, and then do each with your group.

1. **Ask it.** Begin by praying about it, asking God what his plan is, and taking time to really listen to him.

2. **Imagine it.** Ask yourself this question: "What if God ... ?" You fill in the blank. What is something so big that if God isn't in it, it's destined to fail?

3. **Let God expand it.** You've asked for and imagined something big, hopefully really big. Now read Ephesians 3:20: "With God's power working in us, God can do much, much more than anything we can ask or imagine" (*New Century Version*).

Once you know what it is, be sure to crystallize it. Write it down on paper, including all the steps and who will do what. (This is where group members with the spiritual gift of administration can help. Let them use their gifts!)

Your GSP will undoubtedly involve serving others in some way. But you, as a leader, have already started serving your group by including them in all the planning. That's great, because one of the best ways you can serve is to share leadership with others in the group. When you do, you'll impact your group, your church, and the world! More on that in the next chapter.

TALK ABOUT IT

Take a first crack at writing a possible GSP for your group. This may not end up being the real thing, but get the process started.

TRAIT #5
Share

Sharing is a fundamental concept. Most of us learned how to do it in kindergarten. So why do so many people still struggle with it?

Sharing is also an elementary aspect of small group life. I've been alluding to it throughout this book. The fact is, if you've surrendered "your" leadership to God, you'll find it natural to share leadership with others. If you are shepherding group members toward spiritual growth, you'll realize that as you guide them toward Christlikeness, you are moving them onward to servant-leadership. And as I mentioned in the last chapter, if you are truly serving the group, you will let them do some of the leading.

Learning to share happens in three stages: promoting partnership, building teamwork, and breeding leadership.

PROMOTE PARTNERSHIP

On a group mountain bike ride, we were rolling alongside a creek when my front tire hit a deep rut, throwing me off. My bike fell about eight feet toward the creek. I went down after it, of course, but then could get neither myself nor my bike up the creek's steep, muddy embankment. Fortunately, my friend, David, was right there to pull me up. It reminded me of a favorite Bible verse:

Two are better than one,
 because they have a good return for their work:
If one falls down,
 his friend can help him up.
But pity the man who falls
 and has no one to help him up!

(Ecclesiastes 4:9-10).

I've learned a lot about the Christian life on my bicycles. I used to ride alone most of the time, but I've learned that group rides are best! I like having others there to pick me up. I enjoy encouraging one another and pushing each other to go farther, faster, and more dangerously! I love the return for our work when several of us on our road bikes take turns at the front of a pace line as the others draft and get a break. Drafting is a cycling technique that utilizes the laws of aerodynamics to create a wake behind the lead rider, but, even more so, it utilizes the laws of partnership.

Two are better than one on the road, on the trail, and all along the journey. I see the same principles at work in healthy small groups.

- When groups ride through life together—not just attend meetings together—life is better. God created us to live life in partnership with others.

- We need others to "pick us up." In group life, we need to become less independent, yet not unhealthily dependent on each other. The aim is a healthy interdependence, a partnership.

- When individuals take turns at the front and everyone plays a part in the group's work, a tremendous, synergistic return for the work results.

- We should have pity—compassion—for the person who does not have this kind of community.

The next step in learning to share is to build teamwork.

BUILD TEAMWORK

I was selected as the biggest Michael Jordan fan in Anderson, Indiana, in 1993, the year of M.J.'s first retirement. I was selected mostly because I had named my first son after him—well, kind of. My son's name is Jordan Michael; he was born during the 1992 NBA Playoffs and watched his first game with me that same night at the hospital. I like Michael Jordan for a reason: I like basketball and he is arguably the greatest basketball player of all time.[17] And yet his first NBA team, the Chicago Bulls, did not win the NBA championship until his seventh season. That's when they assembled a great team around the world's greatest player.

EVERYONE BRINGS SOMETHING TO THE GROUP

Small groups are much like sports teams. One player, or one leader, does not make a winning team. It takes participation by everyone—teamwork.

That's the essence of the apostle Paul's description in 1 Corinthians 12 of the church as a body: "The body is not made up of one part but of many" (v. 14). What goes for the church as a whole also goes for your small group. Although one person may lead as the group's shepherd, each person has a gift to share with the rest of the group. Some may lead in hospitality, others may lead in administration, serving, encouraging, contributing to others' needs, or showing mercy.

We can determine people's gifts, abilities, and interests by wisely choosing one of these three ways:

- The first is to use a gifts assessment tool. These can be valuable, but they're usually not relational, and I believe they can pigeon-hole people. I think better, more organic ways exist to discover gifts in a small group.

- Another way is simply to ask, "What do you enjoy doing? How can you help lead this group? What have you found you're gifted at? What do other people say you're good at?"

- My favorite way to discover gifts is to watch as you live in community together. As the group gets to know one another, people's gifts will start to become obvious— usually to everyone but themselves! Take time at a meeting to affirm each other's gifts. The group tells each person, in turn, what his or her gift is and why each person is an essential part of the team.

As people's gifts become obvious, find ways to utilize them. People can play numerous roles—everything from timekeeper and tension reliever to social planner, service coordinator, and prayer leader.

TEAMWORK DRILLS

I have loved coaching kid's sports teams, especially basketball. One of the most rewarding parts of coaching for me is taking a rag-tag group of kids who don't know one another at the beginning of a season and turning them into a team—a team that works together as one, each using his unique abilities for the good of the whole. A team that wins because five are better than one. It takes a lot of effort to build this teamwork—lots of drills and time spent together, both in and outside of practices and games. I love the way Coach John Wooden said it years ago, and I still share this quote with my teams: "It takes 10 hands to score a basket."

Building a productive team as a small group is much the same. It takes intentional effort, both inside and outside group meeting times. It takes team-building drills such as these:

- Go on a camping or hiking trip together and give each person a specific assignment.

- Play a game such a volleyball, paintball, or a role-playing game against another group.

- Participate in a shared work experience or serving opportunity.

- Identify a common "enemy" or challenge together.

In Chapter 3, in the "Guide Them to Authenticity" section, I showed you how to start your group as a team. Refer back to that section if you're just getting started. In this chapter, I'm assuming you've built your group as a team. Now it's time to work together more productively.

REMOVE THE OBSTACLES TO TEAMWORK

The biggest obstacle to building a team is a leader who will not, or cannot, share. In my years of ministry, I've discovered three main obstacles:

1. **The Heart:** Some leaders have difficulty handing off responsibilities to others. It's either a lack of trust or a need to control, but either way, this attitude asphyxiates the group.

2. **The Habits:** Some leaders simply have not learned to share leadership. When they were asked to lead, they thought it was their job to do everything, so they do. They lead by habit.

3. **The Head:** I've known some leaders who are really good at everything—except building a team. Even though they have exceptional facilitation skills and Bible knowledge, their groups are unhealthy, stagnant, and sometimes struggle to survive. Why? Because group members sense they're not needed. The leader does everything. The rest of the group just attends meetings. They learn a lot from the studies and like other members of the group, and if that's enough to satisfy them they'll stick around, but not much more.

If you have trouble building a team, what is your obstacle?

If it's the *heart,* ask God to help you change your attitude; ask for humility. As I mentioned in Chapter 2, humility precedes surrender. It's not too difficult for a humble leader to surrender control of the group. Begin by asking God to change your heart to be more like Jesus'.

If it's the *habits:*

1. learn the skills of building a highly functioning team

2. change your habit

3. let your group know things are going to be different

4. apologize for not giving them opportunities and responsibilities in the past

5. ask them to remind you to let them be involved

If it is the *head,* you probably need to recognize the issue and simply back off from doing everything. Swallow your pride; other group members may not lead the same way as you. Another attitude you may need to deal with is perfectionism. If that's you, work at becoming perfect at letting others be involved, even if they're not as good as you!

With God's help, you can turn around the situations by removing the obstacles that keep you from building a team. One of the qualities of a great team is that everyone is working together toward a common goal. As a team, be sure to identify your goals—your God-sized plans—together, and then, as a team, just do it!

I've read lots of good books about building teams. My favorite three are:

- *The One Minute Manager Builds High Performing Teams*, Ken Blanchard, Donald Carew, and Eunice Parisi-Carew, William Morrow and Company

- *Doing Church as a Team*, Wayne Cordeiro, Regal

- *Wooden on Leadership*, John Wooden, McGraw Hill.

BREED LEADERSHIP

Joe and Marlene are a happily married couple with kids. Joe works on the loading dock of a trucking company and Marlene works at a fast-food restaurant. Their three children, Hank, Susan, and Kenneth are very bright. The whole family loves Jesus, and each week they faithfully attend church services. They have family devotions together after dinner each evening, and the children don't just sit there and endure it—they look forward to it and participate. Joe and Marlene are proud parents and love their family!

Hank, the oldest, enjoys writing science fiction stories and shares a bedroom with his brother, Kenny. Susan has always been helpful around the house and cares for the family dog. Kenny, while not nearly as studious as Hank or Susan, is a good athlete and enjoys playing basketball and soccer.

What observations would you make about this family? Would you say they are healthy and on the right track?

As Paul Harvey used to say, "Now the rest of the story":

Joe and Marlene have been married 46 years. Joe is 67 and Marlene will be 63 this year. Hank is 43, Susan is 37, and Kenny, the youngest, was a bit of a surprise to Joe and Marlene. He's 29 years old. All three graduated from college.[18]

Now that you know this additional information, what do you think of this family? What do you think needs to change in this home? Why?

One more question: On a scale of one to five, how similar is your small group to this fictional family in terms of being overly dependent on each other?

Avoid Extinction—Guide Group Members to Continued Growth

Small groups are best described as spiritual families. An essential value is that family members grow up and leave home! A family in which the kids never leave home would be considered unhealthy and unnatural.

The same is true of small groups! Producing and sending out new leaders is a natural occurrence in a healthy group. As the group leader—a spiritual parent—you help guide this family to maturity. Newer Christians still need to be on "pure spiritual milk" (1 Peter 2:2). They need to learn the basics of Christianity, led by more mature members of the group. As believers mature, they become ready to eat solid food (1 Corinthians 3:2). As they continue to grow in their faith, they are given opportunities to lead others and eventually to step out to lead their own spiritual families.

This is called multiplication. Multiplication is a natural, fundamental principle of life. Throughout Genesis, God says, "Be fruitful and increase in numbers (multiply)." Jesus' marching orders for his church involves multiplication. What happens to a family or any other organization that does not multiply itself? Like Joe and Marlene's family, first it becomes very dysfunctional and then unhealthy. Eventually it becomes extinct!

As people in your group are growing in their faith, the natural next step is for you to help them step out and lead others. Why? I can think of at least two reasons, one biblical and one developmental:

1. **The Bible describes a process of spiritual growth that results in leading others.** Hebrews 5:11—6:1 assumes that as you are becoming a mature follower of Jesus, you step out to lead others:

    > There is much more we would like to say about this, but it is difficult to explain, especially since you are spiritually dull and don't seem to listen. You have been believers so long now that you ought to be teaching others. Instead, you need someone to teach you again the basic things about God's word. ... So let us stop going over the basic teachings about Christ again and again. Let us go on instead and become mature in our understanding (NLT).

    Circle the words "become mature" toward the end of this passage and then the words, "ought to be teaching others" in the middle. Then connect them with a line. In a healthy environment, becoming mature naturally leads to teaching/leading/discipling others. It's a process God built into all healthy organisms. Healthy things grow, bear fruit, and then multiply.

2. **The best way for your group members to continue growing is for them to step out of their comfort zones and begin leading others.** A new Christian grows rapidly. After a while, however, that growth begins to slow and eventually becomes incremental at best. Individuals can remain in this plateaued state for years—attending small group faithfully every week and yet not growing. To begin to grow spiritually again, they need a challenge that will spur on their growth and make them rely more on God's power. People who have stepped out on faith discover they grow more than ever. The best thing you can do for plateaued group members is to help them step up to lead!

Small groups have accurately been described as "leader breeders." When you emphasize helping people grow spiritually, new leaders naturally rise up. As they participate in team leadership, they will be prepared to lead. If you've done everything else in this book, you won't be able to hold them back!

HOW TO DEVELOP AND DEPLOY LEADERS

The World's Greatest Small Group Leader was, once again, the perfect example for us. He modeled developing and deploying his group members. In his group, all but one was a leader in training.

Jesus began with a goal for their development: to make them into church leaders—"fishers of men." He told them the plan and then executed it. He spent time with them for three years, modeling everything he wanted them to learn. Over time, they became a team. He gave them opportunities to lead along the way and allowed them to make mistakes. Each time they were involved in servant leadership, he met with them afterward to debrief. He used those opportunities to teach them valuable lessons on leadership. Finally, he sent them out with a mission. As they stepped out to lead, he stayed available for them when they needed him. He promised he would never leave them.

In his book *Transforming Leadership*, Dr. Leighton Ford said, "Long before modern managers, Jesus was busy preparing people for the future. He wasn't aiming to pick a crown prince, but a successor generation. When the time came for Him to leave, He did not put in place a crash program of leadership development—the curriculum had been taught for three years in a living classroom."

Jesus provided guidelines for you as you discover, develop, and deploy leaders:

1. **From the beginning, have a plan for their development.** Have a clear picture in your mind of what you hope they will become.

2. **Tell them the plan.** Let them know up-front that they will be sent out to do the same with others. Repeat this step regularly!

3. **Consider everyone a potential leader-in-training.** When you look at their hearts, perhaps some don't look much like leaders yet. Your responsibility is to shepherd and develop them so that they do.

4. **Spend time with them.** There is no substitute for time in community.

5. **Build a team with them.** Share leadership roles.

6. **Give them opportunities to lead** parts of the meeting and carry out other group leadership responsibilities.

7. **Increase leadership opportunities over time.** Allow them to make mistakes.

8. **Always debrief a leadership experience.** Provide positive feedback and helpful critiques.

9. **As you work as a team together, watch for teachable moments.** Use these to help them grow in servant-leadership.

10. **Send them out.** Continue to be available to them as they need help—more involved at first, backing off over time.

PASS THE BATON

I have handed out a baton, the type used in relay races, to every new leader. Each baton has the phrase, "Pass it on" etched upon it.

Three of my kids used to run track, so I've watched a lot of relays. I've noticed several things about these races that I think are applicable to small group leadership:

1. Everyone on the relay team participates.

2. The team spends a lot of time preparing for their handoffs. They have a strategy for how it will happen. A good, clean handoff is vital.

3. The runner receiving the baton begins running before the preceding runner gets to him. He expects the baton; it's not a surprise. He builds up speed and waits for the handoff.

4. The one holding the baton is responsible for making a clean handoff to the next runner.

In small groups, you figuratively pass the baton not because you are finished with the race but to include others in the race! Don't wait to pass your baton when you are concluding your group. Pass it as soon as someone has said yes to being a leader-in-training or core team member. Let them run for a while with it and then pass it to someone else.

Pass out lots of batons! Yours is a different kind of relay team—a team that passes out batons liberally, because the need for more leaders is great! As you do, keep in mind the wise advice of Pastor Wayne Cordeiro in his book, *Doing Church as a Team*: "It may take only a moment to pass a baton, but it takes much longer to pass the heart of the baton."

THE NEED IS GREAT

Earlier I discussed the visionary passage in Matthew 9:35-38. Let's look at it again from a different perspective.

Jesus' compassion for the people in the crowds led him to do something. He didn't just size up the situation, say, "Wow, that's a shame," and keep going. His compassion moved him to action. But not the kind of action many people would take. Jesus' approach was not, "Get 'er done." It was, "Get prayin'!"

The first thing Jesus did was the first thing he always did: he surrendered it to the Father. He told his disciples, "The harvest is so great, but the workers are so few. So pray to the Lord who is in charge of the harvest to send out more workers."

The harvest is still great. And the workers are still few.

I believe many of the workers will be people just like you—not "professionals," but ordinary people who are already in the harvest fields—in their neighborhoods, workplaces, schools, and families. At the ballparks, gyms, coffee shops, and a variety of other places in the world. They are people who could make a tremendous impact on the world by shepherding 10 to 12 people or so in a small group, and not just any group, but a group with God-sized plans.

TALK ABOUT IT

- To whom in your group are you going to pass the baton? Write their names here.

- What's your plan for building more teamwork and multiplying your leadership? Take some time and write it down on a separate sheet of paper.

TRAIT #6
Steward

I often take a break from my work here at my home office to walk back in my woods. I call them mine because of the amount of time I've spent working back there, even though they technically belong to the county. I've blazed a walking and mountain-bike trail through the woods, complete with log jumps, ramps, and other adventures. I routinely maintain the trail and the woods, cleaning up garbage, removing log jams in the creek, and sawing and removing downed trees that block the path.

These woods are not only my refuge, they're my little piece of creation that I get to work. They are my Garden of Eden. I identify with Adam when I'm in my woods. He was given a place like this to enjoy and manage (Genesis 1:26). It was an act of stewardship:

> Let us make human beings in our image, make them
>   reflecting our nature
> So they can be responsible for the fish in the sea,
>   the birds in the air, the cattle,
> And, yes, Earth itself,
>   and every animal that moves on the face of Earth.

—Genesis 1:26, *The Message*

I've thought about this as I've worked in my woods. God created it all and controls it all. But part of his design was to give us stewardship over what is his—to manage it and work alongside him in caring for it. Sometimes as I remove large branches that impede the flow of the creek, I can immediately see a difference in the direction of the water. This might sound silly, but I seek to be in tune with God enough to sense how I can best work together with him to tend to these woods. After all, they don't belong to me or the county. They're his, but I am his partner.

THE STEWARDSHIP MODEL

Jesus was the perfect example of a good steward. It is obvious in the Gospels that he lived his life on Earth as a steward of all God gave him. Of particular interest is how he illustrated stewardship of the small group entrusted to his care. Seven times in John 17:6-19, Jesus referred to the disciples as being his, given to him by the Father while he was here on Earth. He discussed what he came to do: to pass on to them what the Father had given him (vv. 8, 13, 14). He talked about multiplication—that he was leaving them behind and that he was sending them into the world just as he had been sent (vv. 11, 18).

THE WORLD'S GREATEST SMALL
GROUP LEADER SAID . . .

"I have revealed you to those whom you gave me out of the world. They were yours; you gave them to me and they have obeyed your word. Now they know that everything you have given me comes from you. "

—John 17:6-7

114

Jesus' attitude about his small group is reflected in his summation: "None has been lost except the one doomed to destruction" (v. 12). Not only had they not been lost, but they won thousands to Christ just a few weeks later and started a movement that changed the world. That never would have happened if it had not been for Jesus' attitude of stewardship as he surrendered his will to God's eternal purpose (see Ephesians 3:11).

God has a great, eternal purpose for your small group, too. It will be accomplished when you surrender to it as an act of stewardship.

THE STEWARDSHIP GUIDE

Jesus modeled stewardship for us, and he also spent a lot of time speaking about it. We generally apply Jesus' teachings on stewardship to money, but that's just a small part of the picture. God wants you to wisely manage *everything* he gives you.

In the parable of the talents in Matthew 25:14-30, Jesus gave a number of guidelines for how you can lead your group as an act of stewardship.

1. The Group Is God's, Not Yours

"A man going on a journey ... called his servants and entrusted his wealth to them" (Matthew 25:14).

You have been called to lead something that does not belong to you. It belongs to the Master who has entrusted you, the servant, with the responsibility to invest into your group members while they are in your care.

As the group shepherd, you have been given a huge trust, responsibility, and privilege. As our main passage puts it: "Be shepherds of God's flock that is under your care" (1 Peter 5:2).

As a small group leader, God has entrusted you with much! He's entrusted you with his men and women, his message, and his mission!

I've discussed being a steward of his people and his mission, but what about his message? The apostle Paul sent this warning to the Galatian leaders: "Let me be blunt: If one of us—even if an angel from heaven! —were to preach something other than what we preached originally, let him be cursed" (Galatians 1:8, *The Message*).

This statement is so important, Paul repeated it a second time: "I said it once; I'll say it again: If anyone, regardless of reputation or credentials, preaches something other than what you received originally, let him be cursed" (v. 9).

The theme of stewarding God's message is repeated elsewhere in Scripture:

- "Not many of you should presume to be teachers, my brothers, because you know that we who teach will be judged more strictly" (James 3:1).

- "Let the word of Christ dwell in you richly as you teach and admonish one another *with all wisdom*" (Colossians 3:16, emphasis added).

- "You must teach what is *in accord with sound doctrine*" (Titus 2:1, emphasis added).

The reason Scripture cautions us about sound teaching is obvious. We are handling the truth. Anyone who leads or teaches any kind of group has a high privilege and responsibility. This does not mean, however, that leaders and teachers must be exceptionally talented, highly educated individuals. The apostles were known as "unschooled, ordinary men" (Acts 4:13).

As you lead, you are responsible not only for the group God has given you and his mission, but to correctly handle the word of truth (2 Timothy 2:15).

2. God Gives in Different Proportions

"To one he gave five bags of gold, to another two bags, and to another one bag, each according to his ability. Then he went on his journey" (Matthew 25:15).

It's interesting that the Master gave different amounts to the different servants. At first that doesn't seem fair. But the Master only gave what each servant was capable of handling ("according to his ability"). Think about it this way: Why would God give you more than you can handle? He promises never to give you beyond what you can bear (1 Corinthians 10:13). That's better than fair. That's his grace at work!

God already knows the capacity of our hearts. So he gives generously to the one with the big heart, because he knows that this servant is most capable, spiritually, to bring a bigger return. But he gives the poor steward the minimum amount because he is not as capable to handle the larger responsibility; his heart capacity is smaller.

Each one of the servants acted in accordance to the capacity of his heart. If you want God to entrust you with more—more group members, more influence, more friends, etc.—you need to increase your heart capacity in that area! That begins with what you learned in Chapters 1 and 2—seeking and surrendering to him!

3. God Settles Accounts

"After a long time the master of those servants returned and settled accounts with them" (v. 19).

The events in this parable will actually happen someday. You and I will stand before the Master and we will be held accountable for how we handled what God blessed us with (see Matthew 12:36; 2 Corinthians 5:10; and Hebrews 4:13). God expects a good ROI (Return On his Investment). He expects more than what he left us with. The apostle Paul reminds us, "Yes, each of us will give a personal account to God" (Romans 14:12, NLT).

When you stand before the Master, what do you think he will ask you? I don't know for sure, but if he asks about the group he entrusted you with, he may ask questions like these:

- Did it grow?

- Are members more spiritually mature than when you started with them?

117

- Are they living more abundantly?

- How did you invest your life into theirs and how did they, in turn, invest into the lives of others?

- Did you share ownership and leadership of the group with them?

- Did any of them step up to become leaders?

- Did you multiply the ministry of your group or bury in the ground what God entrusted to you?

My hope and prayer for you is that someday, when you stand before the Master, ready to receive that crown of glory that will never fade away, that his response to you will be, "Well done, good and faithful servant! Well done!"

4. God Judges You on Your Faithfulness

"Well done, good and faithful servant! You have been faithful with a few things; I will put you in charge of many things" (Matthew 25:21).

God will not judge you on what you have done or not done. He will not judge you on your abilities or skills. He'll judge you someday on your faithfulness to him, on your stewardship.

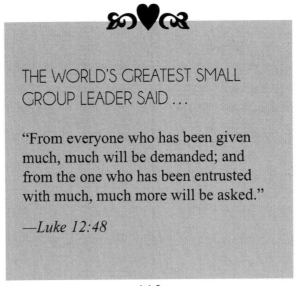

THE WORLD'S GREATEST SMALL GROUP LEADER SAID . . .

"From everyone who has been given much, much will be demanded; and from the one who has been entrusted with much, much more will be asked."

—*Luke 12:48*

That means he will also judge you on your lack of faithfulness. I think it's fascinating that the poor steward said, "I was afraid, so I hid …" (v. 25, NLT). Sound familiar? Adam said the same words in the Garden of Eden when he sinned (Genesis 3:10). That too was a sin of poor stewardship. God had entrusted the Garden to Adam's care and cultivation with only one condition. Adam decided to do things his way rather than God's way.

The result of this lack of faithfulness—this poor stewardship, this sin—is fear and inauthenticity. We've been hiding ever since.

5. God Gives and Takes Away!

"For whoever has will be given more, and they will have an abundance. Whoever does not have, even what they have will be taken from them" (Matthew 25:29).

God gave Adam and Eve the Garden ... and he took it away from them when they were not good stewards of it. The Master gave the last servant something in which to invest ... and he took it away when the man buried it in the ground.

God has given you a group of people to invest into. He will either give you more, if you are good and faithful in your stewardship, or he will take it away if you aren't. If he takes it away, he will give those group members to a good and faithful group leader.

I see this happen in the church all the time. One group leader complains, either because he started with only a few people or because no one stays.

Another leader doesn't know what to do with all the people God keeps sending. She starts with a good-sized group and then even more come. She subgroups so everyone can be involved and shares leadership with everyone in the group, and they keep coming!

The group doesn't close its doors—that would be like burying what God has given them! People keep growing and the more they grow the more people they bring. They serve as a team together, which increases the capacity of their hearts even more. They go and tell people who are lost, like sheep without a shepherd, and they come too! People are leaving other groups to come to this one.

God is giving to them abundantly—more than they can even ask or imagine! The group members, as well as the houses where they meet, are overflowing!

They keep investing and inviting—inviting and investing. They multiply the group not once, not just three times, but, eventually, a hundred times over!

And all this works together to carry out Jesus' mission and bring glory to God.

We have one additional trait to discuss, one that I've learned more about over the last several years. We must continue to do these things over the long run, even as we face trials, obstacles, and difficult circumstances in life and in leadership.

I want to help you as a leader to overcome these struggles and to stand firm!

TALK ABOUT IT

What are the most vital differences between the two groups discussed in this last section?

What heart attributes of the leader are necessary to develop a group like the one that grows and multiplies?

What will it take for your group to bear this kind of fruit?

TRAIT #7
Stand

07/06/2012

Psalm 42

I'm feeling sadder and more hurt, scared, heartbroken, and lost than ever before this morning. So this was a good psalm for me to read today. I feel like everything is crumbling around me and I feel beat up and completely broken. I don't feel like I deserve all this. I'm trying to trust God, but if things keep going as they are, I'm going to lose even more than I've already lost. ...

I feel so overwhelmed by all this. I feel so lost and hurt. I spent a half hour sobbing this morning. My sister called, and I couldn't talk to her. I feel like I have no hope. ...

I wrote those words as I journaled in my Bible app. I was reading through the book of Psalms purposely. I needed them. I desperately needed the reassurance and hope that many of the psalms provide.

I'm opening my life to you here because I know that many readers can relate to my story. The details don't matter much; my wife and I almost lost our marriage, and I'll leave it at that. What is significant is not all the specifics, but how God used this struggle to teach us and develop his life inside of us, so that he can use our lives as only he can for his kingdom purposes. As I said, I was at a place in my life where I felt no hope. But let me finish:

> ... but I know God is my hope. I know I have hope in an eternal life with him and I know I have an abundant life from Jesus now. But I have so many concerns. I guess I need to go back and read Matthew 6 again. (I just did.) I know I shouldn't worry about tomorrow, but I do need to have some plans for tomorrow, right? I do want to keep putting God's kingdom first, knowing he will take care of the rest. I know God has supplied: I have a car that was given to me. I still have this house. I have some money saved in the bank, just in case. I have four good kids. I have some good friends.
>
> God says that when I delight in him, he'll give me the desires of my heart. I want to hold onto that promise. It's just that right now I'm not seeing it. It seems like the desires of my heart are being torn away from me. It's hard to keep trusting as more and more gets taken away, undeservedly I feel.
>
> I've been fighting the good fight. I know there is spiritual battle involved here and I have to keep fighting with the Holy Spirit's power and wisdom. I can't give up! I need to focus on others, not myself, in the midst of this. I will continue to trust in God and take joy in him. I will fight against Satan's attacks because that is where this is coming from. I won't back down.

During this dark valley I learned more about God, myself, relationships, and life than at any other time in my life. In this book's final chapter, I will share some of what I've learned about standing strong even when the circumstances of life are difficult. This chapter was not in the original book, *I'm a Leader ... Now What?* I discovered these vital life principles several years after I wrote that edition.

The fact is, as a Christ follower and Christian leader you *will* face trials. But I want to teach you how to "consider it pure *joy* ... whenever you face trials of many kinds" (James 1:2, my emphasis). The half-brother of the World's Greatest Small Group Leader said those words, and I believe Jesus had a strong impact on James's attitude.

Jesus also influenced his key mentee, Peter, in this regard. Jesus knew Peter would face lots of trials as the early church's go-to leader. Years later, Peter reminded the church, "Be truly glad. There is wonderful joy ahead, even though you have to endure many trials for a little while" (1 Peter 1:6, NLT).

It almost sounds as if James and Peter heard these words from the same person ... because they did!

As Christ followers and Christian leaders, we need to hear and pay attention to these words:

> Dear friends, don't be surprised at the fiery trials you are going through, as if something strange were happening to you. Instead, be very glad—for these trials make you partners with Christ in his suffering, so that you will have the wonderful joy of seeing his glory when it is revealed to all the world (1 Peter 4:12-13, NLT).

Peter later explained a huge part of the reason we can be glad and even joyful in the midst of our troubles: "The Lord knows how to rescue the godly from trials (2 Peter 2:9). As you and I go through the trials and hard circumstances of this life, we must remember that God knows how to get us out of them! I saw him do it in my own life. God rescued me and my wife. He resurrected our relationship. He restored our marriage. Perhaps best of all, he redeemed all of the pain for his glory. God specialized in rescue, resurrection, restoration, and redemption!

STAND IN FAITH

Jesus knew what it was like to face trials in life. The writer of Hebrews reminds us that he is not "unable to empathize with our weaknesses" (4:15). He faced temptations in the desert at the beginning of his ministry and trials in the Garden and at the Cross at the end of it. In the middle, he had to deal with the hard hearts of the religious leaders and

125

the hard heads of his followers. Yet he stood strong through it all—strong in his relationship with his Father, strong as he carried out the Father's will.

Many of our trials in life are related to dealing with people. As someone has said, "Ministry would be easy if it weren't for people!" You might say the same about your small group at times. Jesus had to deal with trials of many kinds within his group. While Jesus' small group did become the World's Greatest Small Group, at times it looked more like a dysfunctional mess!

Within two pages in my Bible, Jesus had to ...

- rebuke his leader-intern (Mark 8:33). Actually, this verse says he looked at all the disciples as he addressed Peter: "You do not have in mind the things of God, but the things of men"

- deal with Peter missing the bigger vision during their mountaintop experience (9:5-6)

- stop an argument between some of his group members and the religious leaders (9:14-16)

- rescue his group members when they couldn't do what he had told them to do (9:18, 25-28)

- correct his disciples who were arguing about which of them the greatest (9:33-34; also see 10:35-45)

The next time you grumble about tensions and problems in your group, look again at Jesus' group!

While Jesus' group was a mess and often dysfunctional, it was healthy. That might seem like an oxymoron, but Jesus understood the principle of *process*. He saw not only what they were, but what they were becoming. And often this process of becoming looks very messy. But think about this: Jesus' dysfunctional group became the World's Greatest Small Group!

If your group is a mess—if your group includes a bunch of dysfunctional, sinful, pride-laden, argumentative men and women—

don't give up! Ask God to help you see the process of what your group members are becoming. At the proper time—God's time—you will reap a harvest if you do not give up!

That takes standing on faith, as Jesus did. Jesus was also teaching— teaching by example—these men in his group to stand firm when they had to deal with opposition. Because they certainly would.

TAKE YOUR STAND EVEN WHEN PEOPLE HATE YOU

When Jesus sent out his small group to minister to people, he gave them authority, specific instructions, and some warnings (see Matthew 10). It appears that the disciples, who had just become apostles, were in the early stages of group life when they were sent, so they didn't have all the answers yet. Imagine you were one of them that day as Jesus gives you instructions and you pack your bags—and then he tells you to leave your bags at home (v. 10). Imagine how you feel as he says:

> "I am sending you out like sheep among wolves" (v. 16).

> "Be on your guard; you will be handed over to the local councils and be flogged in the synagogues" (v. 17).

> "You will be hated by everyone because of me" (v. 22).

> "When you are persecuted in one place, flee to another" (v. 23).

I'd be whispering to the guy next to me, "What in God's name have we gotten ourselves into?"

But Jesus reassured them, as he reassures us: "Do not be afraid of those who kill the body but cannot kill the soul. Rather, be afraid of the One who can destroy both soul and body in hell" (v. 28).

Wait ... what? Kill the body? Destroy the soul? Hell?

Who is going to get us out of this mess? The secret is in verse 40: "Anyone who welcomes you welcomes me, and anyone who welcomes me welcomes the one who sent me." Jesus was promising them something he would promise again and again. Even in the midst of trials and troubles, he would be present with them to the very end. He would not leave them or forsake them. It was a matter of faith:

"You will be hated by everyone because of me, but ..."

But is an important word here, as it is throughout the Bible. As you read through the Psalms, for instance, watch for that three-letter word that signifies faith being put into action. It works this way: *Here are my current crummy circumstances and they feel really terrifying ... BUT ...*

" ... but the one who stands firm to the end will be saved" (v. 22).

Don't miss the "but" of faith in your circumstances! Stand firm to the end because God's got a plan! He knows how to get you out of them.

Take Your Stand against the Devil

As a Christ-following leader you must understand the real source of all these troubles, issues, and haters:

Stay alert! Watch out for your great enemy, the devil. He prowls around like a roaring lion, looking for someone to devour (1 Peter 5:8, NLT).

In the middle of my struggles in 2012, I came to understand rather quickly where many of the problems were emanating. Satan works in a variety of ways and even through unsuspecting people to attack us. His end game is to defeat us and our faith; he comes to steal, kill, and destroy (John 10:10a). He connives, confuses, and corrupts. He lies to us to turn us against God and one another. If you succeed in your Christian faith or as a small group leader, he'll build you up to blow you up. (It's happened too often to too many Christian leaders.)

What can you do?

> Stand firm against him, and be strong in your faith (1 Peter 5:9, NLT).

The apostle Paul would agree with Peter. Paul had gone through more trails and troubles than I can even imagine going through, and yet he kept climbing back up onto his feet and standing strong against external and internal forces. He kept fighting the good fight until the end. He told the church,

> Be strong in the Lord and in his mighty power. Put on all of God's armor *so that you will be able to stand firm against all strategies of the devil* (Ephesians 6:10-11, NLT, my emphasis).

This image of standing firm as you fight against the devil is vital for you to understand, especially as leaders. To remain standing as you fight in a battle means you're staying alive, yes, but it also means you're continuing to wage war for the Kingdom and for the King. Putting on our armor means we are fully trusting in God's strength as we wage war against the enemy, knowing we will stand on the battlefield when the fighting is over (v. 13). We stand our ground (v. 14) against Satan and his evil angel army so that in the end we will remain standing.

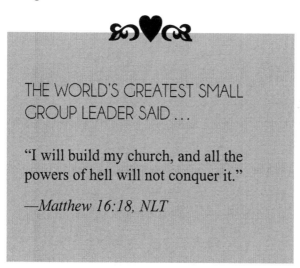

THE WORLD'S GREATEST SMALL
GROUP LEADER SAID . . .

"I will build my church, and all the powers of hell will not conquer it."

—*Matthew 16:18, NLT*

Remember, leader, you and your group are the body of Christ—you are the church—and absolutely nothing, not even Satan and his demon army, can defeat it.

STAND ON THE GOOD NEWS

"Gospel" is a rendering of the Greek *evangelism*, that is, "good message." As a Christian, and especially as a Christian leader, you must stand on this good message. Paul said,

> Now, brothers and sisters, I want to remind you of the gospel I preached to you, which you received and *on which you have taken your stand.* By this gospel you are saved, if you hold firmly to the word I preached to you. Otherwise, you have believed in vain (1 Corinthians 15:1-2, my emphasis).

Standing on the gospel is, of course, tightly related to standing in faith, but this one puts a particular emphasis on the *telling* or *sharing* of that faith with others. Paul often reminded his readers to not be ashamed of this gospel message, but to proclaim it boldly, as he did even when in chains.

Take your stand on the gospel, by which you were saved and for which you carry out Christ's mission. Don't be ashamed to stand up for what you believe, no matter what people say or do in response.

STAND IN GRACE

As we saw, Peter wanted to encourage the church to stand firm in the faith as they resisted Satan (1 Peter 5:9), but he also wanted to remind them of another vital principle:

> My purpose in writing is to encourage you and assure you that what you are experiencing is truly part of God's grace for you. Stand firm in this grace (v. 12, NLT).

Grace simply means that you and I get what we don't deserve (and we don't get what we do deserve). We get God's love. We receive God's forgiveness. We experience God's presence with us. God listens and responds to our prayers. We can approach God's throne of grace with confidence because of ... well, his grace. We get to lead others purely because of grace. God works in and through us in extraordinary ways because of his grace. We earn none of it. We get to be part of all this because Jesus took what we deserve (and what he didn't deserve) at the cross.

Are you approaching God in prayer based on your own worthiness or on grace?

Are you standing in your own power or in God's grace?

Are you leading in your own strength or by God's grace?

Stand firm in God's grace.

STAND IN THE TRUTH OF GOD'S WORD

I was mountain biking with four friends when we came to a log roll on an uphill section. A log roll is simply several logs on the trail that you need to cross. This particular obstacle has always been difficult to get over, but now the approach into it was severely washed out, making it seemingly impossible to get over the logs. I thought I'd found a way, however, by going to the left where the ground was still somewhat intact, but to cross the log at that location meant I needed to then work through a couple of other obstacles, as well. I thought I could make it. My riding buddies, however, didn't think it could be done. They even pointed out the reasons why. But here's my secret: I saw chain-ring marks on top of the log in that location, meaning other people had made it before. It could be done.

Often we allow ourselves to think, "I can't get through this," "This is impossible," or "It's too difficult." Even our friends see the obstacles and chime in, "Don't even try," "Take the easy way out," or "It's too dangerous for you." It happens all the time, it seems—in our marriages, in unplanned pregnancies, among church pastors, in small groups.

I introduced this chapter with my journal entry from Psalm 42 and how I was feeling about my personal, seemingly unsurmountable obstacles at that time. The author of the psalm was facing similar obstacles and journaling his feelings and thoughts in those circumstances:

> Why am I discouraged?
>> Why is my heart so sad?
> I will put my hope in God!
>> I will praise him again—
>> my Savior and my God! (vv. 5-6, NLT).

The first two lines describe how the psalmist (and I) *felt*, which is based on what he had been *thinking* about. Our emotions start in our minds—on what we choose to focus. The good news is that God can change the way you think (Romans 12:2)! The rest of the verse is based on the writer's *will*.

God created us with emotions—the human ability to feel and sometimes feel very deeply. Our emotions have many wonderful benefits; they are, after all, a part of what make us human. The Greatest Commandments involve our feelings: to *love* God and others. The fact is, however, that your emotions are not reliable. Also, don't forget that your emotions are not some independent force in your life. I often hear people try to explain their poor choices by saying they *felt* it was the right thing to do at the time—even when the decision went square against sound biblical principles and good common sense! You and I are responsible for our feelings and what we do with them (see James 1:13-15; Ephesians 4:26).

I've learned that I often need to set my feelings aside and allow my will to take over. I decide that I *will* put my hope in God and I *will* praise him again. These decisions are not necessarily based on how I feel or even what I think. Look at the next verse in Psalm 42 and the same pattern:

> Now I am deeply discouraged [how he *felt*], but I *will* remember you (v. 6, NLT, comment and emphasis added).

There's another example of a biblical "but" of faith!

If you are to stand strong in your faith, against the devil and his schemes, throughout difficulties, you must stand on something that is firm, strong, reliable, and everlasting. That solid ground is not your emotions and often not even your thoughts (since your thoughts can be influenced by others as well as by Satan).

Jesus had and often expressed human emotions. He showed anger toward the teachers of the Law (and yet did not sin) and grief at the grave of his friend Lazarus, for example. As Satan tempted Jesus in the wilderness, Jesus' human emotions must have been exhausted. He had fasted forty days, so imagine how that would have affected him emotionally. Yet each time the devil tempted him, Jesus responded with Scripture. Jesus knew how to stand firm in his faith: stand on the truth of God's Word.

Look at how the disciple Jesus loved said it:

> Our actions will show that we belong to the *truth*, so we will be confident when we stand before God. Even if we *feel* guilty, God is greater than our feelings, and he knows everything (1 John 3:19, 20, NLT, emphasis added).

Indeed, God is greater than our feelings, and he expresses his plan and will for us in his Word. The Bible reveals the Good News about our eternal life in God's kingdom and shows us how to live life to the full right now. The apostle Paul reminded us, "But you must continue to believe this truth and *stand firmly in it*. Don't drift away from the assurance you received when you heard the Good News" (Colossians 1:23, NLT, my emphasis).

That's great advice for you and me as we live and lead others. God's Word is more than just a book—it is a wonderful resource we need to live the Christian life well. It is a resource that must be paired, however, with another resource for your faith.

STAND IN THE POWER
OF THE SPIRIT

God's Word and God's Spirit work hand in hand. The apostle John often called the Holy Spirit the "Spirit of truth" (John 14:17; 15:26; 16:13; 1 John 4:6; 5:6). The Spirit partnered with human writers to produce the Scriptures; he guides people into truth (16:13), teaches the truth, and reminds us of the truth Jesus taught (16:26).

THE WORLD'S GREATEST SMALL GROUP LEADER SAID . . .

"But now I am going away to the One who sent me, and not one of you is asking where I am going. Instead, you grieve because of what I've told you. But in fact, it is best for you that I go away, because if I don't, the Advocate won't come. If I do go away, then I will send him to you. And when he comes, he will convict the world of its sin, and of God's righteousness, and of the coming judgment."

—John 16:5-8, NLT

Before he went to the cross, Jesus told the disciples what they needed to know most, and a prominent part of his talk revolved around the Holy Spirit, whom he promised to them when he left. In the beginning of John 16, we find Jesus once again warning his followers about the persecution they would soon face. Yet he told them it would be better for him to physically leave them, because then the Holy Spirit would come and be with them, working in front of, in, and through them.

Jesus' words in John 16 are vital for you and me as leaders. He shows us how dependent we must be on the Holy Spirit as we exercise leadership in his church. The Spirit empowers us for Christ's mission (Acts 1:8), directs us in his mission (8:29-39; 13:2; 16:6-7), and provides the gifts we use in carrying out his mission.

Don't miss this. You are utterly dependent on the Holy Spirit to do anything worthwhile in ministry. He inspires, invigorates, instructs, and, well, inspirits you for the mission he initiates.

As a group, be sure to follow the advice of the apostle Paul and "stand firm in the one Spirit, striving together as one for the faith of the gospel without being frightened in any way by those who oppose you" (Philippians 1:27-28).

The Leader of the World's Greatest Small Group made an astonishing announcement just before going to the cross. He is speaking to you and your group here, if you simply believe in him: "I tell you the truth, anyone who believes in me will do the same works I have done, and even greater works, because I am going to be with the Father" (John 14:12). He went on to say that you can ask for anything in his name and he will do it, but there's a condition on that: it must be something that brings glory to the Father (see vv. 13-14).

If you and your group SEEK first God's Kingdom, if you SURRENDER your own purposes for his, if you SHEPHERD the group under your care in God's ways, if you faithfully and unselfishly SERVE others and SHARE group ownership and leadership with others, living as a STEWARD of what God has given you, and if you continue to STAND even when things get tough, here's Jesus' promise:

YOUR GROUP CAN BECOME THE WORLD'S GREATEST SMALL GROUP!

Your group can do even greater things because you have the power of the One who led the way and is the way, the truth, and the life.

STAND UNTIL THE END

The apostle Paul came to a time when he knew his life in this world—and therefore his earthly ministry—was short. Yet he knew he had fought the good fight and finished the race (2 Timothy 4:6-8). I believe we all want to be able to make that kind of statement at the end of this life. Just to know we left it all on the field, we held nothing back in this life, we left this existence with no regrets.

Paul encouraged the Corinthian church about the resurrection in 1 Corinthians 15. He wanted them to have complete assurance of the Christian's resurrection based on Christ's resurrection from the dead. Yet that encouragement had a specific application for them—and us—in the here and now. He said, "Therefore, my dear brothers and sisters, *stand firm*. Let nothing move you. Always give yourselves fully to the work of the Lord, because you know that your labor in the Lord is not in vain" (v. 58, my emphasis).

Yes, your resurrection is coming, perhaps sooner than you think. Yes, Jesus died and rose again to give you eternal life. Yes, Jesus has already prepared a place for you in heaven. Yes! But he's not done with you yet. He has a plan for you as long as you are breathing. So give yourself fully to his work, because, rest assured, your labor is not in vain.

What a promise! You may not see the fruit of your work for him during this lifetime, but as long as you stay connected to the Vine, he will bear fruit through you.

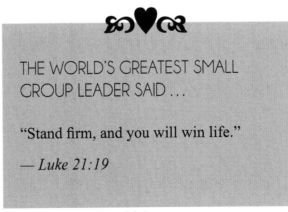

THE WORLD'S GREATEST SMALL
GROUP LEADER SAID . . .

"Stand firm, and you will win life."

— *Luke 21:19*

James reminded his readers of the same truth: "You too, be patient and stand firm, because the Lord's coming is near" (5:8). Your labor is not in vain.

I know that leading a small group can get tiring. Don't give up.

I know your group may be a dysfunctional mess. Group members are flawed, foolish, flaky, and feckless. Love them anyway.

I know Satan has attacked, is attacking, or will attack you. If you are carrying out Christ's mission, you are his enemy. Stand firm in your faith and in your all-powerful God of angel armies.

I know. I do. I've been there myself. But that's not really important.

What is important is this: God knows. Not only does he know, but he is standing with you ... always, to the very end of the age.

So, with nothing to fear, go! Go and be the group God desires for you to be: The World's Greatest Small Group!

TALK ABOUT IT

Throughout this book we've talked about the capacity of leaders' and group members' hearts, which can be measured by seven vital traits. These were the heart attributes of the World's Greatest Small Group Leader, as well.

Measure the capacity of your heart using the following scales. Be honest!

1 = a tiny heart, like the worthless servant in the parable of the talents (Matthew 25:14-30)

5 = a big heart, like the World's Greatest Small Group Leader

Seek	1	2	3	4	5
Surrender	1	2	3	4	5
Shepherd	1	2	3	4	5
Serve	1	2	3	4	5
Share	1	2	3	4	5
Steward	1	2	3	4	5
Stand	1	2	3	4	5

How are these interrelated?

Where do you need to grow most right now?

What's your first step?

Notes

[1]*Leadership*, Spring 1995.

[2]Joel Comiskey, *Home Cell Group Explosion* (Houston, Texas: TOUCH Outreach Ministries, 1998), 26-36.

[3]Ibid, 34.

[4]Bill Thrall, Bruce McNicol, and Ken McElrath, *The Ascent of a Leader* (San Francisco: Jossey-Bass Publishers, 1999), 81.

[5]John Fischer, "Under New Ownership," The Purpose Driven Daily Devotional, August 17, 2005. http://www.purposedrivenlife.com.

[6]Henry and Richard Blackaby, *Spiritual Leadership* (Nashville: Broadman & Holman Publishers, 2001), 43.

[7]These graphics adapted from Campus Crusade for Christ International, http://www.ccci.org.

[8]Warren Wiersbe, *Bible Exposition Commentary—New Testament, Volume 2* (ivictor.com, 2002, in WORDsearch, 2005), chapter 8.

[9]Ralph W. Neighbour, Jr., *The Shepherd's Guidebook*, rev. ed. (Houston, Texas: TOUCH Outreach Ministries, 1996), 34.

[10]John Ortberg, *Everybody's Normal Till You Get to Know Them* (Grand Rapids, Michigan: Zondervan, 2003), 18.

[11]Neighbour, 67.

[12]This list taken from the text of *Leadership by the Book* by Ken Blanchard, Bill Hybels, and Phil Hodges (New York: William Morrow & Company, 1999), 42, 43.

[13]Warren Wiersbe, *Bible Exposition Commentary—New Testament*, Volume 1 (ivictor.com, 2002, in WORDsearch, 2005), chapter 18.

[14]Jim Petersen, *Living Proof,* fourth printing (Colorado Springs: NavPress, 1991), 120.

[15]Quoted on an e-mail listserv from evangelist Reinhard Bonnke.

[16]This list is a collection of material I've compiled from various sources. The framework and some of the contents came from a Willow Creek Small Group Conference.

[17]Michael Jordan led the NBA in scoring ten times (an NBA record), including seven straight times from 1987-1993. He has the highest career points per game average, holds the record for most seasons leading the league in scoring—10, shares the record for the most consecutive seasons leading the league in scoring—7, and had a streak of nine consecutive games scoring 40 points or more. He was the Most Valuable Player five times, Defensive Player of the Year (1988), steals leader three times, nine-time All-Defensive First Team (1988-93, 1996-98), Rookie of the Year (1985), fourteen-time all-star, All-Star MVP three times, all-time scoring leader in All-Star history, won the All-Star Slam Dunk Contest two times, and two-time Olympic gold medalist. http://www.nba.com/history/players/jordan_stats.html; http://www.23jordan.com/stats1.htm; http://en.wikipedia.org/wiki/Michael_Jordan

[18]This story is excerpted from my ebook, *Leaving Home, A Small Group Parable for Making Disciples into Disciple Makers,* available at https://smallgroupleadership.com/product/leaving-home-a-small-group-parable-for-making-disciples-into-disciple-makers/.

[19]Wayne Cordeiro, *Doing Church as a Team* (Ventura, California: Regal, 2001), 114. Cordeiro is senior pastor at New Hope Christian Fellowship in Honolulu, Hawaii.

More information about World's Greatest Small Group:

https://smallgroupleadership.com/worlds-greatest-small-group

Discuss the book ...
- On Goodreads: www.goodreads.com/book/show/33285211-world-s-greatest-small-group
- On Amazon

Other Books by Michael C. Mack ...
http://smallgroupleadership.com/product-category/books/michaelsbooks
- *Small Group Leader Toolbox: Everything You Need to Lead a Thriving Small Group* (eBook)
- *Leaving Home: A Small Group Parable for Making Disciples Into Disciple Makers* (eBook)
- *Small Group Vital Signs: Seven Indicators of Health that Make Groups Flourish* (TOUCH)
- *The Pocket Guide to Burnout-Free Small Group Leadership: How to Gather a Core Team and Lead from the Second Chair* (TOUCH)
- *Leading from the Heart: A Small Group Leader's Guide to a Passionate Ministry* (TOUCH)

Studies by Michael C. Mack
http://smallgroupleadership.com/product-category/studies/michaels-studies
- *Launch Into Community Life: Building a Master Plan of Action with Your Small Group* (TOUCH)
- *Moving Forward: Helping Your Group Members Embrace their Leadership Potential* (TOUCH)

Connect with Michael
- *Webpage:* www.smallgroupleadership.com
- *Facebook:* www.facebook.com/SmallGroupLeadership
- *Twitter:* twitter.com/michaelcmack
- *Instagram:* www.instagram.com/michaelcmack
- *LinkedIn:* www.linkedin.com/in/michaelcmack
- *Pinterest:* www.pinterest.com/michaelcmack

Made in the USA
San Bernardino, CA
20 June 2017